Happy All

HAPPINESS
IS A
CHOICE

Grateful and Joyful Comes
From You Alone

Rivera Hill

Table of Contents

PART 1

Chapter 1:

Happy People Consciously Nurture A Growth Mindset

"Without continual growth and progress, such words as improvement, achievement, and success have no meaning." – Benjamin Franklin

Learning is perceived and generally acknowledged by those of us who have gone through primary and university tutoring. We were routinely encircled by people who energized and upheld our developments. Groundbreaking thoughts and change were anticipated from us; the sky was the limit!! However, shouldn't something be said about once we got into the work environment? For some, we subsided into the everyday daily practice, getting it done, uninformed of the cost that our agreeable, monotonous, continuous tasks appeared to have on our own and expert development.

Do you hear employees saying, "I don't get how this venture's development works" or "I'm awful at giving introductions. If it's not too much trouble, let another person do it." If this is the case, reconsideration of your group's growth mindset might be in order. They are working under a "fixed mentality." According to an examination concentrate via Carol Dweck of Stanford University, a fixed attitude happens when individuals accept fixed qualities that can't change. These individuals archive abilities instead of attempting to foster them. On the other hand, a development attitude accepts that knowledge can develop with time and experience. When individuals accept they can add to their learning, they understand exertion affects their prosperity.

You can attempt to battle a fixed attitude and energize a sound growth mindset by rehearsing the following:

Recognize fixed mindset patterns

To begin with, would you say you are ready to precisely recognize and uncover the negative quirks coming about because of a fixed mentality? Normal practices of these individuals incorporate the individuals who keep away from challenges, surrender effectively, consider there to be as achieving nothing, overlook and keep away from negative criticism, need heading in their objectives, and carry on when feeling undermined by other people who make progress. These are normal signs that employees are battling to see their part in supporting the new turn of events.

Energize feedback over praise

Commendation feels better. We like to feel approved in our qualities and are content to let it be the point at which we get acclaim over achieved work—employees to request input despite the result. There are consistent approaches to improve and create. Lead your group to request tips and innovative manners by which they can move toward new situations.

Pinpoint skills and limitations

Take time out from the ordinary daily schedule to pinpoint your workers' qualities and shortcomings will give an unmistakable beginning stage to an initiative in realizing where holes exist. Have workers independently take strength evaluations and meet with them to go over outcomes. Some may feel compromised and cautious while going over shortcomings, yet having a direct discussion on the finding will prompt better anticipation and recuperating.

Happy People Create Time to Do What They Love Every Day

Most of our days are filled with things that we need to do and the things we do to destress ourselves. But, in between all this, we never get time for things. We wanted to do things that bring us pure joy. So then the question is, When will we find time to do what we love? Then, when things calm down a bit and when the people who visit us leave or finish all the trips we have planned and wrap up our busy projects, and the kids will be grown, we will retire? Then, probably after we are dead, we will have more time.

You do not have to wait for things to get less busy or calmer. There will always be something coming up; trips, chores, visitors, errands, holidays, projects, death and illness. There is never going to be more time. Whatever you have been stuck in the past few years, it will always be like that. So now the challenge is not waiting for things to change it is to make time for things you love no matter how busy your life is. Sit down and think about what you want to do, something that you have been putting off. What is something that makes you feel fulfilled and happy? Everyone has those few things that make them fall in love with life think of what is that for you. If you haven't figured it out yet, we will give you some examples, and maybe you can try some of these things and see how that makes you feel.

- Communing with nature

- Going for a beautiful walk

- Creating or growing a business or an organization

- Hiking, running, biking, rowing, climbing

- Meditating, journaling, doing yoga, reflecting

- Communing with loved ones

- Crafting, hogging, blogging, logging, vlogging
- Reading aloud to kids
- Reading aloud to kids

Did you remember something you enjoyed doing, but as the responsibilities kept increasing, you sidelined it. Well, this is your sign to start doing what you loved to take time out for that activity every day, even if it is for 30 minutes only. Carve that time out for yourself, do it now. Once you start doing this, you will realize that you will have more energy because your brain will release serotonin, and your energy level will increase. Secondly, your confidence will improve because you will be making something love every day, and that will constantly help you gain confidence because you will be putting yourself in a happy, self-loving state. You will notice that you have started enjoying life more when you do something you love once a day. It makes the rest of your day brighter and happier. You will also want to constantly continue learning and growing because your brain will strive to do more and more of the thing you like to do, and that will eventually lead to an increased desire of learning and growing. Lastly, your motivation will soar because you will have something to look forward to that brings you pure joy.

Chapter 2:

How to Face Difficulties in Life

Have you noticed that difficulties in life come in gangs attacking you when you're least prepared for them? The effect is like being forced to endure an unrelenting nuclear attack.

Overcoming obstacles in life is hard. But life is full of personal challenges, and we have to summon the courage to face them. These test our emotional mettle — injury, illness, unemployment, grief, divorce, death, or even a new venture with an unknown future. Here are some strategies to help carry you through:

1. Turn Toward Reality

So often, we turn away from life rather than toward it. We are masters of avoidance! But if we want to be present—to enjoy life and be more effective in it—we must orient ourselves toward facing reality. When guided by the reality principle, we develop a deeper capacity to deal with life more effectively. What once was difficult is now easier. What once frightened us now feels familiar. Life becomes more manageable. And there's something even deeper that we gain: Because we can see that we have grown stronger, we have greater confidence that we can grow even stronger still. This is the basis of feeling capable, which is the wellspring of a satisfying life.

2. Embrace Your Life as It Is Rather Than as You Wish It to Be

The Buddha taught that the secret to life is to want what you have and do not want what you don't have. Being present means being present to the life that you have right here, right now. There is freedom in taking life as it comes to us—the good with the bad, the wonderful with the tragic, the love with the loss, and the life with the death. When we embrace it all, then we have a real chance to enjoy life, value our experiences, and mine the treasures that are there for the taking. When we surrender to the reality of who we are, we give ourselves a chance to do what we can do.

3. Take Your Time

As the story of the tortoise and the hare tells us, slow and steady wins the race. By being in a hurry, we actually thwart our own success. We get ahead of ourselves. We make more mistakes. We cut corners and pay for them later. We may learn the easy way but not necessarily the best way. As an old adage puts it: The slower you go, the sooner you get there. Slow, disciplined, incremental growth is the kind of approach that leads to lasting change.

Happy People Are Optimistic

Beyond the simple reality that optimists are happier people (and happiness is what you're striving for), optimism has other benefits as well. So, if you want to achieve greater happiness, try being optimistic for a day.

Optimists enjoy a greater degree of academic success than pessimists do. Because optimistic students think it's possible for them to make a good grade, they study hardier and they study smarter. They manage the setting in which they study and they seek help from others when they need it. (Optimism, it turns out, is almost as predictive of how well students do in college as the SAT.)

Optimists are more self-confident than pessimists are. They believe in *themselves* more than fate.

Optimists are more likely to be problem-solvers than pessimists are. When pessimistic students get a D on a test, they tend to think things like: "I knew I shouldn't have taken this course. I'm no good at psychology." The optimistic student who gets a D says to herself, "I can do better. I just didn't study enough for this test. I'll do better next time." And she will.

Optimists welcome second chances after they fail more than pessimists do. Optimistic golfers always take a *mulligan* (a redo swing without penalty). Why? Because they expect to achieve a better result the second time around.

Optimists are more socially outgoing than pessimists are. Socially outgoing folks believe that the time they spend with other human beings makes them better in some way — smarter, more interesting, more attractive. Unfortunately, pessimists see little, if any, benefit from venturing out into the social world.

Optimists are not as lonely as pessimists are. Because pessimists don't see as much benefit from socializing with others, they have far fewer social and emotional connections in their lives, which is what loneliness is all about.

Optimists utilize social support more effectively than pessimists do. They aren't afraid to reach out in times of need.

Optimists are less likely to blame others for their misfortune than pessimists are. When you blame someone else for your troubles, what you're really saying is, "You're the *cause* of my problem and, therefore, you have to be the *solution* as well." Optimists have just as many troubles as pessimists throughout life — they just accept more responsibility for dealing with their misfortune.

Optimists cope with stress better than pessimists do. Pessimists worry, optimists act. A patient with coronary heart disease who is pessimistic "hopes and prays" that he doesn't have another heart attack anytime soon. The optimistic heart patient leaves little to chance — instead, he exercises regularly, practices his meditation exercises, adheres to a low-cholesterol diet, and makes sure he always gets a good night's sleep.

Chapter 3:

10 Habits of Serena Williams

Serena Williams is one of the greatest tennis players of all time. To win 23 grand slams, she had to overcome obstacles that most tennis players don't face: she is a black woman in a predominantly white sport, grew up in a poor neighbourhood that was not always safe, she endured intense scrutiny of her body, racism, and misogyny.

Despite this, she still manages to be an exceptional tennis player. Williams has epitomized the grit, resilience, and mental toughness required to overcome every obstacle and hardship she has had to endure since the beginning of her career, hence inspiring athletes worldwide.

Here are 10 habits of Serena Williams for your life lessons.

1. Make Your Path

Your path is unique to you and only you. Serena has never followed a script. She was raised in Compton, California, trained by her father, mostly eschewed the junior circuit-the traditional path to tennis success. Her emergence on the scene as a teenager player to embracing her physical prowess and chiselled figure says it all. She told Robin Roberts in an interview that she is only up to win, and inspire people.

2. Adapt Well

To maintain success, you must welcome change. Adaptability includes the ability to recover rapidly from adversity. Serena Williams demonstrates her adaptability by playing on the scorching hot hard court of the Australian Open, the slick clay of the rainy French Open, and the quick grass of Wimbledon. That implies that she delves deep when necessary.

3. Enjoy the Moment

When it comes to stressful situations, Serena enjoy seizing the opportunity to differentiate herself from the competition. Does she ever doubt herself? Yes! She accepts it, bottle it up, and toss the bottle away. Her mind-set is one that you can grasps.

4. Fuel a Work-Life Balance

Bring your entire being to everything you do. Serena's work-life balance is well-documented: she is a minority owner of the Miami Dolphins, makes her clothing and footwear, heads charity, and is a wife and mother. These outlets shape who she is as a person, and maintaining a healthy balance translates into complete focus and performance.

5. Fight Till the End

Serena has made it a point never to give up. She fights till the end in everything she does, and it has led to her incredible success. Nothing seems to break her! Coming from a poor upbringing, she has fought her way to the top. You may not be able to move or serve as she does, but you can always fight as she does.

6. Focus

Williams once stated, "if you can keep playing tennis when someone is shooting a gun down the street, that's focus!" Thanks to the tough times in her Compton upbringing, Serena has been focusing her way up to success.

7. Have Faith

Serena Williams' self-assurance over the tennis courts has allowed her to dominate. Her physique is not that of a "typical thin tennis player," but she accepts herself regardless while inspiring and encouraging other women. Having faith in every possible way in your life keeps you dominating and moving.

8. Shake It off Sooner

After qualifying for the Australian Open in 1998, Serena didn't have the best opening match, as she lost the first set. But she was not going down without a struggle. Her outstanding comebacks since then are well renowned. It's not over yet, just be present! You're still in it, and you'll have to battle for it.

9. Don't Give a Damn What Others Think

Williams has faced a lot of sexism and racism, mainly because of her physical appearance, which has been a significant factor in her domination. She has always been vocal on such criticism as well as encouraging women facing similar scepticism to heed not to what is said. As an aspiring female athlete, you can't afford the terror of being defined as "having too many muscles" and being mocked or labelled unattractive bring you down.

10. Believing in Oneself Can Be a Lonely Endeavour

People always doubted Serena's return after child delivery. But she always stated on several occasions that ignoring the odds and what others think is a critical component of overcoming hurdles and ultimately reaching success. When no one else believes in you, you have to believe in yourself.

Conclusion

Just like Serena Williams, no matter what your life's circumstances are, as an aspiring athlete or whatever your situation, keep your focus intact. Stay strong and always find a way of being a winner.

Chapter 4:

"Happy People Enjoy the Hidden Pleasures life has to offer."

It is said that the best things in your life are free, and there is not even a shred of doubt in that life is filled with satisfying hidden pleasures. To feel fulfilled, you need to enjoy them, so we are going to list some of the most simple, satisfying hidden pleasures life has to offer so that next time when you find yourself in a similar situation, you take out a moment and truly enjoy it:

Finding money you did not know you had: Reaching into your pocket and finding out a dollar 20 bill from the last time you went out wearing those jeans brings absolute joy all of a sudden. You have some extra money on you that you completely forgot about.

Receiving a Real letter via snail mail: Since email is more used these days, it has become the primary source of written communication, and most of the things you find in your snail mail are junk. So, when you find a package or a letter from someone you know in the mail, it brings joy, and a sense of excitement takes over you as you start opening the gift.

Making Brief Eye Contact with Someone of the Opposite Sex: We are all so busy in our lives, and most of the times when we are out, we spend time looking at our screens, so sometimes there is a rare moment where you pass them in a subway or street, and they look at you momentarily making direct eye contact that communicates a subtle curiosity, and for a second you think about it and then it's just gone.

Saying the Same Thing Simultaneously: Sometimes, you and your friend notice something or react to something by yelling out the same set of words. This is something that occurs rarely, but it gives you something to smile about.

Realizing You Have More Time to Sleep: Sometimes, you abruptly wake up in the middle of the night, and you think it's time to wake up, and when you look at the time, and you still have two more hours to sleep. A warm euphoric feeling shoots through your body at that moment, and then you glide back to your dreams.

The feeling after a healthy workout: There is a feeling of self-satisfaction and accomplishment that you get; this is one activity that will make you feel better and also make you look good at the same time. So when you walk out of the main door of the gym, you feel like you are on top of the world.

Relaxing Outdoors on a Sunny Day: When you are relaxing in your chair, reading your favourite book as the light breeze keeps the temperature under control, and the sun warms your skin, you feel at peace with the environment around you.

Making Someone smile: Sometimes you notice that your fellow student is under great stress due to the exams that are just coming up, so you invite them over to your place to just relax, have good food and watch a movie with a smile on their face as they enjoy yourself will make you the happiest.

Chapter 5:

Chapter 6:

Everything is A Marathon Not A Sprint

Ask your parents, what was it like to raise children till the time they were able to lift their weight and be self-sufficient. I am sure they will say, it was the most beautiful experience in their lives. But believe me, They are lying.

There is no doubt in it that what you are today is because of your parents, and your parents didn't rest on their backs while a nanny was taking care of you.

They spent countless nights of sleeplessness changing diapers and soothing you so that you can have a good night's sleep. They did that because they wanted to see a part of them grow one day and become what they couldn't be. What you are today is because of their continuous struggle over the years.

You didn't grow up overnight, and your parents didn't teach you everything overnight. It took years for them to teach you and it took even more time for you to learn.

This is life!

Life is an amalgamation of little moments and each moment is more important than the last one.

Start with a small change. Learn new skills. The world around you changes every day. Don't get stuck in your routine life. Expand your horizons. What's making you money today might not even exist tomorrow. So why stick to it for the rest of your life.

You are never too old to learn new things. The day you stop learning is the last day of your life. A human being is the most supreme being in this universe for a reason. That reason is the intellect and the ability to keep moving with their lives.

You can never be a millionaire in one night. It's a one-in-billion chance to win a lottery and do that overnight. Most people see the results of their efforts in their next generation, but the efforts do pay off.

If you want to have eternal success. It will take an eternity of effort and struggles to get there. Because life is a marathon and a marathon tests your last breaths. But when it pays off, it is the highest you can get.

Shaping up a rock doesn't take one single hit, but hundreds of precision cuts with keen observation and attention. Life is that same rock, only bigger and much more difficult.

Changing your life won't happen overnight. Changing the way you see things won't happen overnight. It will take time.

To know everything and to pretend to know everything is the wrong approach to life. It's about progress. It's about learning a little bit at each step along the way.

To evolve, to adapt, to figure out things as they come, is the process of life that every living being in this universe has gone through before and will continue to go through in the future. We are who we are because of the marathon of life.

Every one of us today has more powerful things in our possessions right now than our previous 4 generations combined. So we are lucky to be in this world, in this era.

We have unlimited resources at our disposal, but we still can't get things in the blink of an eye. Because no matter how evolved we are, we still are a slave to the reality of nature, and that reality is the time itself!

If you are taking each step to expect a treat at each stop, you might not get anything. But if you believe that each step that you take is a piece in a puzzle, a puzzle that becomes a picture that is far beautiful and meaningful, believe me, the sky is your limit.

Life is a set of goals. You push and grind to get these goals but when you get there you realize that there is so much more to go on and achieve.

Committing to a goal is difficult but watching your dreams come true is something worth fighting for.

You might not see it today, you might not see it 2 years from now, but the finish line is always one step closer. Life has always been and always will be a race to the top. But only the ones who make it to the top have gone through a series of marathons and felt the grind throughout everything.

Your best is yet to come but is on the other end of that finish line.

Chapter 7:

10 Habits of Mariah Carey

Mariah Carey has earned not only a "diva" reputation but also a legendary pop icon for over 30 years in the spotlight. She's an American singer-songwriter, actress, and record producer who has lauded her as a "songbird supreme" and the "queen of Christmas." Despite a challenging start, her debut album charted no. 1 in the US, went multi-platinum, and earned her Grammy Awards for Best Female Vocalist and Best Artist. She is one of the most successful female performers of all time, with more than 200 million albums sales landing her a net worth of $320 million. Her distinctive acute euphonies and melismatic runs continues shaping pop music up to date. If you're wondering how this simple New York girl climbed up to becoming this legendary, this is for you! Here are the ten habits of Mariah Carey.

1. Made the Most of What She Was Good At

According to Mariah Carey, she discovered her singing strengths at the age of 6 when her friend, whom she was singing with while holding hands, surprisingly stopped to listen to her. It was from this moment she realized that she had something exceptional and devoted to it. Knowing your strength and devoting entirely to it will eventually land you a lucky spot.

2. Leave No Doubt

Taking your game to the next level can be daunting, and it takes confidence to do so. Mariah Carey's career began magically, but it wasn't long before trolls and haters sprouted. Trolls accused her of being "studio warm" because her voice was so flawless, to be true. She was so troubled by such critics that she decided to shock her detractors with a live performance on MTV.

3. Passion Never Goes Wrong

When Mariah decided to ditch her pop image to focus on R&B and Hip Hop, her decision, as she mentioned in an interview, did not sit well with her record label at first. But eventually resulted to a breakthrough album that is still regarded as the best to date. That's what happens when you believe in your abilities and take a stand for them. Simply put, you're the one who knows how far your abilities can stretch.

4. Forget Plan B, Go Hard on Plan A

To meet your success, you need one well-thought-out plan. With a well-organized plan, make decisions that are in line with your ultimate success objectives. Mariah Carey's music was her life and she was serious and ambitious. Go all in and carry out your only plan as if your life depended on it.

5. Persistence

Perseverance, not talent, is the secret to success. "I knew in my heart that one day I'd make it... Every day that I made it through, I knew I was getting closer to my goal. "Every night, I would thank God for the day when I didn't give up or be knocked down," Carey said in an interview. When you are ambitious, pushing hard is core to achieving your goals.

6. She's All About Equality

If you have a platform, use it to propel influence against societal injustices. Carey received the GLAAD Ally Award in 2016 for her support of the LGBT community. She once assisted one of her backup dancers in proposing to his boyfriend on stage. According to GLAAD CEO Sarah Kate, Mariah Carey has always inspired and encouraged numerous LGBT admirers worldwide with her unwavering commitment to acceptance and inclusive campaigns.

7. A Little Downtime Won't Harm

Mariah mentioned her prior husband's mental and emotional abuse, as well as the chaotic filming of Glitter, in an interview. She worked 22 hours a day, which harmed her mental health and led to her hospitalization in 2001. Your lofty goals demand a healthy mind and body.

8. Explore Constantly

Allow yourself to make mistakes and explore without feeling obligated to deliver a saleable piece every time. Because of Mariah's daring explorations, Male-female collaborative raps and melodies were created by hip hop artists. There's a lot more, but the bottom takeaway is that Maria Carey's daring approach to music paid off.

9. Dream Big

You don't need to know how you'll accomplish the tremendous success you want for yourself; all you need to know is that it will happen. Carey envisioned herself taking off the music industry without doubt and also surpassing Joan Crawford's manor's splendour.

10. Follow Your Superiors

If opportunities don't come knocking at your door, make a door. When Mariah first started recording demos in high school, she met older and more experienced musicians than her. And boy, did she learn! It's also where she worked with Brenda K. Starr, a Puerto Rican freestyle singer. It was through the star that she got noticed by big bosses.

Conclusion

Of course, you don't need to follow suit completely, but you can learn from the divas herself that faith, desire, perseverance, and how serious you take your dreams important manifestation tools.

Chapter 8:

Becoming a Leader

Wow today we're going to talk about a topic that i think might not apply to everybody but it is one that is definitely interesting as well and good for everyone to know if they some day aspire to be a leader of sorts.

Leadership is something that does not come naturally to everyone, while some are born leaders as they say, in reality most of us requires life experiences, training, and simply good people skills in order to be an effective leader that is respected.

To be a respected leader, you have to have excellent communication skills who come across as fair and just to your employees while also being able to make tough decisions when the time comes.

I believe that leaders are not born, but their power is earned. A person who has not had the opportunities to deal with others on a social and business level can never be able to make effective decisions that serves the well being of others. A leader in any organisation is one that is able to command respect not by force but by implicit authority.

So what are some ways that you can acquire leadership skills if you feel that you lack experience in it? Well first of all i believe that putting yourself in more social and group settings in friendly situations is a good place to start. Instead of jumping right into a work project, you can start by organising an activity where you are in charge. For example those that involve team work and team games. Maybe an escape room, or even simply taking charge by organising a party and planning an event where you become the host, and that usually means that you are in charge of getting things in order and all the nitty gritty stuff. Planning parties, coordinating people, time management, giving instructions, preparing materials... All these little pieces require leadership to pull off. And with these practices in events that will not affect your professional career, after you get a good feel of what it is like, you can move on to taking on a leadership role in projects at school or work. And hopefully over time all these practices will add up and you will be a much more holistic leader.

Soft skills are a key part to being an effective leader as well. Apart from professional expertise at the work place. So i encourage you to be as proficient in your learning of people skills and mastering interpersonal communication as well as being fluent in all the intricacies and details of your job description.

If you require a higher level of leadership training, i would encourage you to sign up for a course that would put you in much more challenging situations where you will be put to the test. This may be the push that you need to get you on your path to be the leader that you always thought that you could be.

Personally, I have always been a leader, not of a team, but of my own path. That instead of following in the footsteps of someone, or taking orders from bosses, i like to take charge of what i do with my time. And how to manage my career in that fashion. As much as i would like to tell myself that i am an effective leader, more often that not, i can honestly say i wish i was better. I wish i was better at managing my time, at managing my finances, at managing my work, and I have to always upgrade my leadership skills to ensure that I am effective in what I do. That I do not waste precious time.

Your leadership goals might be different from mine. Maybe you have an aspiration to be a head of a company, or division, or to lead a group in charitable work, or to be a leader of a travel tour group. Being a leader comes in all forms and shapes, and your soft skills can definitely by transferable in all areas.

So i challenge you to take leadership seriously and to think of ways to improve your leadership skills by placing yourself in situations where you can fine tune every aspect of your personality when dealing with others. At the end of the day, how people perceive you may be the most important factor of all.

I hope you learned something today, take care and as always, i will see you in the next one.

Chapter 9:

Happy People Dream Big

Remember being a kid, and when somebody asked you what you wanted to be after growing up, you answered with a big dream: an astronaut, a ballerina, a scientist, a firefighter, or the President of the United States. You believed that you could achieve anything you set your mind at that no dream is too big that if you wanted, you would make it happen. But why is it that so many adults forget what it is like to dream big. Happy people are dreamers; if you want to become a happy person, you need to make dreaming big a habit; some people even say that if your dreams do not scare you, you are not dreaming big. Now you must be wondering how dreaming big can make you happy. Firstly, it helps you see that if you had a magic wand and you could get whatever you wanted, what you would want for yourself, and there is a chance that these dreams are things you want to achieve in your life somehow other. Secondly, it will help you in removing any fears you have about not being able to achieve your dreams because when you dream big, you think about what you want in your ideal world, and your fear will not come in your way because you would feel like you are living in that fantasy world. Lastly, you will put your dreams and desires into the universe, and the likelihood of making those dreams come true increases. Fulfilling your dreams makes you happy because you will be able to get what you have yearned for so long, and a sense of achievement will make you feel confident about yourself and the dream you had. Now you must have a question what should I do to start dreaming big I am going to outline some of the things you can practice!

Sit back, clear your mind and think about your desires and dreams. What do you want in life? If you had three wishes from a genie, what are the things you would ask for? What is something you would if no one was looking or if you weren't afraid. Now write these dreams down on a piece of paper. This way, they would seem more real. The next thing you should do is start reading some inspirational books that motivate you to start living your best life starting today! Lastly, make a list of goals you want to achieve and start working on them.

Happy People Choose to Exercise

There is a feeling you get when you just finish your workout, and you feel amazing, much better than you were feeling before. Even when you are not feeling motivated to go to the gym, just thinking about this feeling makes you get up, leave your bed and get going to the gym. This feeling can also be called an endorphin rush. Exercise indeed makes you happier in multiple ways.

Firstly, movement helps you bond with others that are in the brain chemistry of it all. Your heart rate is going up, you are using your body, engaging your muscles, your brain chemistry will change, and it will make it easier for you to connect and bond with other people. It also changes how your trust people. Research also showed that social pressures like a hug, laughing, or high-five are also enhanced. You will also find your new fitness fam, the people you will be working out with, and because you will have a shared interest that is having a healthy lifestyle will help you have a stronger bond with them. And as experts say that having strong relationships and connections in life will help you in overall happiness.

We have already discussed those exercise increases endorphins but what you do not know is that it increases a lot more brain chemicals that make you feel happy and good about yourself. Some of the brain chemicals that increase are; dopamine, endorphins, endocannabinoid and adrenaline. All of these chemicals are associated with feeling confident, capable, and happy. The amount of stress, physical pain, and anxiety also decrease significantly. A chemical that your body creates when your muscles contract is called "myokine", it is also shown to boost happiness and relieve stress.

Secondly, exercise can help boost your confidence, and of course, when it comes to feeling empowered and happy, confidence is the key. "At the point when you move with others, it's anything but a solid feeling of 'greater than self' probability that causes individuals to feel more idealistic and enabled, "Also, it permits individuals to feel more engaged turning around the difficulties in their own lives. What's more, that is a fascinating side advantage of moving with others because there's an encapsulated feeling of 'we're in the same boat' that converts into self-assurance and the capacity to take on difficulties in your day; to day existence."

Thirdly, exercising outdoors affects your brain, similar to meditation. In case you're similar to the innumerable other people who have found out about the advantages of contemplation yet can't make the time, uplifting news. You may not need to contemplate to get a portion of the advantages. Researchers found that exercising outside can similarly affect the cerebrum and disposition as reflection. Exercising outside immediately affects a state of mind that is amazingly incredible for wretchedness and nervousness. Since it's anything but a state in your mind that is the same as contemplation, the condition of open mindfulness,"

Chapter 10:

Why You're Demotivated By A Values Conflict

Every human being, in fact, every organism in this universe is different from even the same member of their species. Every one of us has different traits, likes, dislikes, colors, smells, interests so it's natural to have a difference of opinion.

It's natural to have a different point of view. It's natural and normal to have a different way of understanding. And it's definitely normal for someone else to disagree with your ways of dealing with things.

Most of us don't want to see someone disagreeing with us because we have this tricky little fellow inside of us that we call EGO.

Our ego makes us feel disappointed when we see or hear someone doing or saying something better than us. We cannot let go of the fact that someone might be right or that someone might be Okay with being wrong and we can't do a single thing about it.

This conflict of values occurs within ourselves as well. We want to do one thing but we cannot leave the other thing as well. We want to have something but we cannot keep it just because we don't have the resources to maintain them.

This feeling of 'want to have but cannot have' makes us susceptible to feelings of incompleteness ultimately making us depressed. The reality of life is that you can't always get what you want. But that doesn't make it a good enough reason to give up on your dreams or stop thinking about other things too.

Life has a lot to offer to us. So what if you can't have this one thing you wanted the most. Maybe it wasn't meant for you in the first place. Nature has a way of giving you blessings even when you feel like you have nothing.

Let's say you want something but your mind tells you that you can't have it. So what you should do is to find alternative ways to go around your original process of achieving that thing and wait for new results. What you should do is to give up on the idea altogether just because you have a conflict within your personality.

You cannot let this conflict that is building within you get a hold of you. Clear your mind, remove all doubts, get rid of all your fears of failure or rejection, and start working from a new angle with a new perspective. Set new goals and new gains from the same thing you wanted the first time.

This time you might get it just because you already thought you had nothing to lose.

This feeling of 'No Regret' will eventually help you get over any situation you ever come across after a fight with your inner self. This feeling can help you flourish in any environment no matter what other people say or do behind your back.

Nothing can bring you peace but yourself. Nothing holds you back but your other half within you.

PART 2

Chapter 1:

Happy People Savor the

Moment

Learning to "savor the moment" in life is a convenient, free, and effective way to increase your happiness and quality of life and reduce stress. Enjoying what you have can help you to appreciate what you've got rather than lamenting what you don't have and creating stress by striving for too much. Being able to savor the moment with loved ones can bring a stronger connection and sense of appreciation, which leads to better quality relationships and all the benefits of social support that they bring. Learn more about these techniques to savor the moment in life.

1. Focus on Details

Sometimes as we go through life, we forget to stop and enjoy the little things; indeed, it's possible to go through an entire day either stuck in your ruminations about the past or anxious over the future, never really seizing the moment and noticing the pleasant things that are happening right now (and passing up positive opportunities right and left). As you savor the moment, notice the little things that can make a day special — the smile of a friend, the kindness of a stranger, the beauty of a sunset

2. Focus on Sensations

As you're experiencing your day, notice and memorize the details — especially the positive details — of what's happening around you. Create a memory. Notice the sounds you hear, like the sound of children's laughter in the background. Notice the smells, like the scent of a fresh sea breeze. And how did that wind feel on your face? Noticing these types of sensory details helps you live fully in the moment and can help evoke pleasant memories when you hear music, smell aroma, or feel sensations you experience on the days you want to savor.

3. Focus on the Positive

As humans, we're naturally wired to notice the negative events in life more than the positive, as these are what we need to keep track of to maintain our safety: if we're aware of threats around us, we're more able to launch a defense. However, if we actively focus on the positive, we can stress less and enjoy life more from an increasingly optimistic vantage point. To savor the moment, notice what's going right, and appreciate it. This isn't the same as pretending you're happy when you're not; it's more about noticing the things that lead to greater happiness and reduced stress.

4. Express Gratitude

Feeling gratitude goes along with noticing the positive and is an excellent way to savor the moment. Notice all the nice things that people do for you (and thank them whenever possible), or simply notice what you enjoy about people when they're just themselves (and be sure to tell them that, too). Appreciate what goes right in your day as it happens, and write it down in a gratitude journal at night — it's a surprisingly effective way to both raise your level of daily gratitude and build a record of all the things in your life that can make you happy when you're having a bad day.

Chapter 2:

When To Listen To That Voice Inside Your Head

Everyday we hear a voice in our head telling us things to us. Whether it be a negative voice telling us not to do something, or a positive one that pushes us to try something new, we sometimes forget when and when not to listen to it.

Today I found myself in that very situation. I found myself walking going about my day when I heard a voice telling me that I should go back to my passion, which was to record music, and simply used my voice as the only tool to make music. I had heard this voice many times before, but i always brushed it away because I thought to myself, no one is going to want to hear me sing. Why should anyone? My voice sucks. It's not as good as other people. No one is going to like it. And I am just going to waste my time. Those negative voices always found a way to beat down my positive one to the point where I just gave up listening to them altogether because I figured that I was never going to act on anything out of my fears to do so anyway.

But something happened today that made me listen. Today I felt like it had a point to make and it was trying to get out. and today those goblin voices that usually tried to kill that positive one was silent. I took that opportunity to head straight down to the nearest electronics store, to buy an expensive mic, and decided that I was going to pursue this venture no matter what. I wanted to do it for myself. I wanted to do it because I didn't want to regret not listening to that inner voice 10-20-30 years down the road. Sure people might still not listen to me sing, but dammit i was going to do it anyway.

It didn't matter to me if only 5 people liked it. It mattered more that I liked it. It mattered more that I overcame myself and finally put music out there that I was proud of.

I bought that mic because I didn't want the excuses in my head to start creeping up on me again. I bought that mic because it gave me no way out. I was already committed. And if I didn't do it I would've just wasted a ton of money. Sometimes in life you have to push yourself and give no reasons to turn back. Because it is always easy just to give up. But when that object is staring at you, sitting and calling out to you, you are going to one to use it.

We all have voices in our heads that tell us to do something crazy but magical in our lives. We shove them aside because we are afraid. We shove them aside because we don't dare to dream. We shove them aside because we think we are not good enough. We fail to realize that we are just one decision away from changing our lives.

Carrie Underwood, for those of you who don't know who she is, she won American Idol in 2005 and became one of the biggest country music superstars in the world. Did you know that she almost didn't make the trip to audition for American Idol because that goblin voice in her head told her it was a stupid idea to go? In that split second decision where she decided to try anyway, it changed her life forever. She changed the music scene forever. It was crazy to think a girl from a small town could win as many Grammys as she did, but she did.

This is the same dilemma you and I face everyday. We fail to realize that everytime we say no to that crazy idea, we are taking one step back in our lives. Soon we become so used to taking these steps back that we end up taking them forever, failing to achieve anything great in the process. Life is simply one giant list of decisions that we make on a daily basis. Any decision that we choose not to take, is a decision that is either missed, or lost.

Start listening to what that voice inside your head has been telling you to do. Has there been something that has been painfully obvious to you? A voice that has been recurring that you've been shoving aside? Take a pen, write that voice down on apiece of paper. Dig into it and start finding out if you should be taking action on it. You never know what that one decision can do for the rest of your life unless you give it a shot.

Chapter 3:

Happy People Stay Present

"Realize deeply that the present moment is all you ever have."

According to a study, 50% of the time, we are not fully present in the moment. We are either thinking about the past or worrying about the future. These things lead to frustration, anxiety, and pain in our daily life. Each morning as soon as we wake up, we start seeking distractions. As we wake up with a clear mind, we should be grateful for a new day that we got; instead, we start looking for our phone, start going through interwebs and rush into our days. So now we are going to help you and list some of the things that will help you stay present.

Stop Being a Slave to Your Mind: For the next four days, let's do an exercise where you pay attention to your thoughts and see what crosses your mind. You. You will soon realize that majority of the thoughts that you have are destructive. There will be very little time to think about the present, and the majority of your thoughts would be about the past or the future. So, whenever this happens and you find yourself wandering consciously, try to bring yourself back to the present. Also, you need to remind yourself that multi-tasking is a myth and focus on one thing only.

Tap into Your Senses: If you mindfully tap into your senses, you will realize that it is a fantastic way of bringing more awareness into your day. Because our eyes are wide open all day, we can see, but we forget to tap into other senses such as taste, touch, or smell. But if you use these, you can feel more present and calm down if you are in a stressful situation. You might not realize this, but our senses play a huge role in manifesting our reality. For example, everything we are hearing we are touching will regularly turn into our reality. That is why we can use the power our senses have and feel more calm and present.

Listen Closely: Everyone loves to talk, but only a few people like to listen. People love to share their dreams, what they have accomplished and what they desire, and still, nobody seems to be listening closely.

"When you talk, you are only repeating what you already know. But if you listen, you may learn something new."

When you listen carefully, you will be able to charm people and at the same time learn new things and be present. Because you will be focusing on what they are saying, you will focus on the current moment. This way, you will also be able to silence your thoughts about the past and future because you will be consciously listening and focusing on what they are saying. This will also benefit your relationship in the long run because when you need an ear to listen to your problems, they will be there for you. This is a win-win situation for you, and you will improve your relationship while practising being more present.

Chapter 4:

Happy People Don't Sweat the Small Stuff.

Stress follows a peculiar principle: when life hits us with big crises—the death of a loved one or a job loss—we somehow find the inner strength to endure these upheavals in due course. It's the little things that drive us insane day after day—traffic congestion, awful service at a restaurant, an overbearing coworker taking credit for your work, meddling in-laws, for example.

It's all too easy to get caught up in the many irritations of life. We overdramatize and overreact to life's myriad tribulations. Under the direct influence of anguish, our minds are bewildered, and we feel disoriented. This creates stress, which makes the problems more difficult to deal with.

The central thesis of psychotherapist Richard Carlson's bestselling *Doesn't Sweat The Small Stuff... And It's All Small Stuff* (1997) is this: to deal with angst or anger, we need not some upbeat self-help prescriptions for changing ourselves, but simply a measure of perspective.

Perspective helps us understand that there's an art to understand what we should let go of and what we should concern ourselves with. It is important to focus our efforts on the important stuff and not waste time on insignificant and incidental things.

I've previously written about my favorite 5-5-5 technique for gaining perspective and guarding myself against anger erupting: I remove myself from the offending environment and contemplate if whatever I'm getting worked up over is of importance. I ask myself, "Will this matter in 5 days? Will this matter in 5 months? Will this matter in 5 years?"

Carlson stresses that there's always a vantage point from which even the biggest stressor can be effectively dealt with. The challenge is to keep making that shift in perspective. When we achieve that "wise-person-in-me" perspective, our problems seem more controllable and our lives more peaceful.

Carlson's prescriptions aren't uncommon—we can learn to be more patient, compassionate, generous, grateful, and kind, all of which will improve the way we feel about ourselves and how other people feel when they are around us.

Some of Carlson's 100 recommendations are trite and banal—for example, "make peace with imperfection," "think of your problems as potential teachers," "remember that when you die, your 'in-basket' won't be empty," and "do one thing at a time." Others are more informative:

- Let others have the glory
- Let others be "right" most of the time
- Become aware of your moods, and don't allow yourself to be fooled by the low ones
- Look beyond behavior
- Every day, tell at least one person something you like, admire, or appreciate about them.
- Argue for your limitations, and they're yours
- Resist the urge to criticize
- Read articles and books with entirely different points of view from your own and try to learn something.

Chapter 5:

When It's Okay to Not Be Okay

Let's be honest, happiness is not something you can "just choose". If It was, then sad moments could not be there. Do not pressure yourself to be happy, because if you do, then you are inadvertently setting a path of the war with yourself. This is why **adopting a mindset that embraces** "not all that happy" feelings we can arise within us is essential for carrying on with a happier life.

In the stumbling on happiness, Daniel Gilbert describes happiness, "There is no basic recipe for happiness." Certainly, it's anything but an objective to accomplish. Or maybe it's the bi-result of carrying on with a wholehearted life - a daily existence wherein we permit ourselves to chance feel the full range of human feeling - dissatisfaction, grief, dismissal, misery, insufficiency - and to accept our battles and to acknowledge our ourselves as the questionable "human becoming" that we are".

We can help ourselves along in that cycle by accomplishing a greater amount of what grows our ability for every one of the encounters and feelings that life holds available.

Here are a 7 Ways To help You Cope and Accept When It's Okay Not to Be Okay.

1. Accept Life's Upsetting Emotions.

Bear this in mind, there are only two types of people who don't usually experience painful emotions; psychopaths and people who've died. Feeling or experiencing sad and painful moments are part and parcel of your life. At any point when you deny, excuse, numb or attempt to obstruct yourself from feeling them completely – something many are profoundly adroit at doing – you are just prolonging your torment and making superfluous suffering.

2. Practice "gently/friendly curiosity"

As human beings, the truth is, we are intrinsically emotional or passionate creatures– occasionally, we act before reasoning. Also, satisfaction – those sentiments bliss, happiness, and connection - is only one of the numerous feelings on the wide enthusiastic range.

The best way to encounter unadulterated snapshots of happiness, connection, appreciation, and love is the point at which you allow yourself to experience sadness, misery, dread, and hurt. Embrace these sad feelings with curiosity. This requires allowing yourself to sit with the less lovely feelings without desensitizing, minimizing, or over-relating to them. As such, "the solitary way out is through."

3. Practice More of Whatever Makes You Stronger — Body, Mind, and Soul.

Since numerous things in your life are out of your control, it bodes well to be proactive in those parts of your life over which we have some proportion of control. Growing day by day customs and propensities to assist you with bringing your "best self" to your greatest difficulties is vital. Eat well, burn some calories, invest your energy with individuals who lift you. Limit time with the individuals who don't. Re-energize your energy, re-focus your soul, and pull together on your first concerns. The little private every day moves you make can lead to large open outcomes that you frequently need.

4. Look at Yourself as a Person Who Is "Human Becoming"

Every time you will see people who seem to have everything in perfect order, and feel they don't encounter any of the battles and uncertainties that you do. It's untrue.

Accepting yourself as a 'human becoming that you are — complete with every one of your inadequacies, fears, and frailty — helps you to grow fully into your humankind and connect all more with that of others.

Everyone at some point in their lives messes up, falls down and up, and fails to be as kind-hopeful patient-restrained as they'd prefer to be. Such is the human condition. Thumping yourself for being human doesn't serve you. This is the reason, in your fallen moments, you should be kinder to yourself. Commit to accepting your flaws or imperfections and acknowledge your mistakes as you move up to healing.

5. Rest Your Sadness

Thinking of sadness as the opposite of happiness is easy, and accordingly, something to be evaded. Truth be told, misery is the feeling that directs you toward what you care about most and is a pathway to happiness. At the point when you cut yourself off from feeling the profundity of your misfortune, from sitting with your misery and distress, you additionally cut yourself off from being available to bliss, close connection, and happiness.

Therefore, allowing yourself ample time to sit with your sadness, let the tears flow-if need be, and be there fully to feel the sad moments-that permitting yourself to fully feel the ache -taking all things together in its rawness - allows you to gradually discover your way back wholly and healing and to getting more deliberate in your work, as a parent, and throughout everyday life. It's an excursion that is continuous.

6. Cultivate Seeds of Gratitude

Happiness cannot be bought from external sources, be it money, success, and fame. It is all on everyone's knowledge that most people who are materially wealthy are profoundly unhappy. Which is true. You should learn to appreciate whatever you have, hence the more appreciation, the happier you will feel. It's the reason we must be purposeful in zeroing in on the things that fuel feelings of appreciation, in any event, when there are parts of our lives that aren't as we'd like.

7. Spend your time offline-take a break from social media

Finally, perhaps the main thing you can do to cultivate happiness and develop your versatility for managing your afflictions is being in a place where there are meaningful relationships. Turning to the right people and connecting with them in realness and during your vulnerable moments is more impactful on your inner peace instead of scrolling down the social media feeds.

In conclusion, it is okay to be vulnerable- it is okay to feel unhappy-it is okay to share the feeling with the right people. Just keep in mind that an unhappy feeling which is felt enough can permanently reside in your psyche and overshadow all others. So, feel what should be felt and afterward be deliberate in investing your time and attention toward whatever re-establishes viewpoint and grows your ability to make a move to make whatever it is you need a greater amount of in your life.

If you found this video helpful, don't forget to like, subscribe, comment, and share this with someone important to you. I hope you learned something valuable today. Take care, have a good rest, and till the next video ☺

Chapter 6:

How To Crush Your Goals This Quarter

Some people find it very hard to achieve their goals, but luckily, there is a method waiting to be used. The quarter method divides the year into four parts of 90-days; for each part, you set some goals to crush. The rest of the year has gone, and so have the three quarters; now it is time to prepare for the fourth quarter. 1st October is one of the most critical days in the life of a person who sets his goals according to the quarter. It is the benchmark representing the close of the third quarter and the beginning of the fourth quarter. It is the day when you set new goals for the upcoming three months; if somehow your third-quarter dreams were not crushed, then you can stage a comeback so you wouldn't be left behind forever. But how to achieve your fourth-quarter goals?

1st October may bring the start of a quarter, but it also ends another quarter; it is the day when you focus on your results. Have you achieved the goals you set for the third quarter? If not, then prepare yourself to hear the hard truth. Your results reflect your self-esteem; if you believe in yourself, then you would achieve your goals. If you are not satisfied with your results, think, is this what you had in mind? If no, then having small visions can never lead to a more significant impact. Limiting beliefs will never give you more than minor and unimpressive results. Your results tell you about your passion for your work; if you are not passionate about your work, you would have poor outcomes. We all have heard the famous saying, " work in silence and let your success make the noise," but what does this mean? It means that your results will tell everyone about your hard work. If your results are not satisfactory, you know that the problem is your behavior towards your work.

When setting goals for the future, one needs to accept the facts; what went wrong that put you off the track? The year is 75% complete, and if you still haven't crushed your goals, you need to accept that it is your fault. If you blame these failures on your upbringing, your education, or any other factor than yourself, then you are simply fooling yourself because it is all dependent on you. When you don't achieve what you wanted to in nine months, you must have figured the problem; it can be any bad habit you are not willing to give up or the strategies you are implying. If you pretend your habits, attitude, and approach are just fine, you are just fooling yourself, not anyone else. This benchmark is the best time to change the old bad habits and try forming some new strategies.

To finish the year with solid results, you need to get serious; the days of dissatisfied results are gone, now it is time to shine some light on your soul and determine what you are doing wrong, what habits are working in your favor, and which ones are not. Then you can decide which habits to give up on, which habits to improve, and which ones to keep. Once you have sorted this out, prioritize your goals and set some challenging destinations to avoid getting bored or feeling uninterested. When setting deadlines, try to set enforceable deadlines.

Confusion can lead to poor results, so sit back and think about the goals that I should not pursue. This is called understanding goal competition; the goals you set are competing for your time. Actual peak performance comes from understanding which goals to pursue and which not to seek. And when you complete a plan, don't just rush into the process of crushing the next goal; allow yourself to celebrate your win and feel the happiness of the goal finally getting destroyed by you.

Chapter 7:

Happy People Have A Morning Ritual

For many of us, mornings begin in a rushed panic. We allow our alarm clocks to buzz at least a dozen times before deciding we have to get out of bed. Then we rush around our homes half-awake, trying to get ready for our day. In a hurry, we stub our toe on the bedpost, forget to put on deodorant, and don't pack a lunch because we simply don't have time. It's no wonder that so many folks despise the thought of being awake before 9 a.m.!

So it may not surprise you to know that the happiest and healthiest people tend to enjoy their mornings. They appear to thrive on waking up with the sun and look forward to a new day of possibilities. These people have humble morning rituals that increase their sense of well-being and give their day purpose.

Here are 3 morning habits that healthy and happy people tend to share:

1. They wake up with a sense of gratitude

Practicing gratitude is associated with a sense of overall happiness and a better mood—so it makes sense that the happiest and healthiest people we know start the day with a gratitude practice. This means that they're truly appreciative of their life and all of its little treasures. They practice small acts of gratitude in the morning by expressing thankfulness to their partner each morning before they rise from bed. They may also write about their gratefulness for five minutes each morning in a journal that they keep by their bedside.

2. They begin every morning anew.

The happiest and healthiest people know that every day is a brand-new day—a chance to start over and do something different. Yesterday may have been a complete failure for them, but today is a new day for success and adventure. Individuals who aren't ruined by one bad day are resilient creatures. Resiliency is a telltale sign of having purpose and happiness.

3. They take part in affirmation, meditation, or prayer.

Many of the happiest folks alive are spiritual. Affirmations are a way of reminding ourselves of all that we have going for us, and they allow us to engrain in our minds the kind of person we wish to be. Meditation helps keep our mind focused, calms our nerves, and supports inner peace. If you're already spiritual, prayer is a great way to connect and give thanks for whatever higher power you believe in.

Happy People Take Care of Themselves

I frequently hear the word "selfish" tossed about in coaching, often with a negative connotation. Someone feels bad that they were selfish or that someone else was selfish, and it was offensive. Selfishness – the lack of considering others or only being concerned with your advantage – can be a great weakness. The ability to put others' needs in front of your own is an important life skill that you need to be able to do without resentment, even when it's completely inconvenient and a sacrifice.

However, I would argue that the motivation behind that decision should be self-serving. In most cases, being selfish is just a matter of perspective, critical to happiness and self-evolution.

Let me explain…

First, let's talk about why it is so important to be selfish. As author <u>Brené Brown</u> has discovered in her research on wholehearted living, loving yourself more than you love others is the first and most critical step to seeking happiness and fulfillment.

She says it is impossible to love anyone more than you love yourself. Taking care of yourself is the pathway to fulfillment and high performance in work and life. And, just as importantly, it's a gift to others.

When your needs are met, and you feel good about yourself, it's easier to elevate other people's needs in front of your own. It's easy to be a giver when your cup is full. When you feel half-full or empty, it's harder to give. You inherently feel people should be giving more to you or others, so you don't have to give so much or feel you need to preserve more for yourself.

Here are the two common derailments that can prevent you from finding fulfillment:

1. Giving too much

When people give too much - continually put other people's needs ahead of their own - builds resentment and takes away from their ability to take care of themselves. When their time is so focused on others, they don't have any time left for themselves. I find people do this when they are uncomfortable asking for their needs, speaking up about issues, or delegating responsibilities. Often they hide these weaknesses by focusing on other people, so they don't have to focus on themselves. This not only leads to feeling unfulfilled but becomes a burden on others who feel they need to take care of the "giver."

2. Taking too much time for ourselves

On the opposite end of the spectrum, some people take too much time for themselves, mistakenly thinking it will lead to fulfillment. They do not "give" enough, and it usually makes them feel worse, disengaging them from relationships and putting them on a treadmill of trying to do something that will finally make them feel good. In these cases, they are usually working on the wrong issues. The places where they are investing their time do not give them meaning.

Chapter 8:

Happy People View Problems as Challenges

To state the obvious: It's easier to be happy when things are going well. Positive outcomes are known to lift people's moods, while negative emotions (like anxiety) generally reflect concerns about negative outcomes.

But, happy people are also good at dealing with problems in ways that help them to maintain their mood, while still dealing with issues effectively. Here are three common things that happy people tend to do to deal with speed bumps in life.

FOCUS ON THE FUTURE

It is important to understand the problem you're facing, and so happy people certainly analyze the situation. But, they don't remain focused on the problem for long. That is, they avoid rumination—which is a set of repeated thoughts about something that has gone wrong.

Instead, they look to the future. There are two benefits to this: One is that the future is not determined yet, and so happy people can be optimistic about things to come. The other is that happy people are looking to make the future better than the past, which creates a hopeful outlook—no matter what the present circumstances look like.

FIND AGENCY

At any given moment, the situation you are in exerts some amount of control over your options. When you're sitting in traffic, for example, there isn't much you can do but wait for the cars around you to start moving. The amount of control you have to take action in a situation is your degree of agency.

Happy people seek out their sources of agency when problems arise. They are most interested in what they can do to influence the situation, rather than focusing on all of the options that have been closed off by what has happened. The focus on agency is important, because it provides the basis for creating a plan to solve the problem. And the sooner a problem is addressed, the less time it has to cause stress.

KNOW WHEN TO FOLD

There are always going to be big problems that you can't solve. Perhaps there is a client who is never satisfied with the work you do. Maybe there is a process you're trying to implement that never seems to have the desired outcome. You might even have been working on the problem for a long time.

Despite all the discussions about the importance of grit, effective (and happy) problem solvers are good at knowing when to walk away from a problem that can't be fixed. Each of us has a limited amount of time and energy that we can devote to the work we are doing. Spending time on problems that cannot be solved has an opportunity cost. There are other things you could be doing with your time that might yield better outcomes. It is important to learn when it is time to give up on a problem rather than continuing to try to solve it.

This is particularly true when you have been working on that problem for a long time. There is a tendency for people to pay attention to sunk costs—the time, money, and energy they have already devoted to working on something. But, those resources are gone, and you can't get them back. If it isn't likely that additional effort is going to help you solve a problem, then you should walk away, no matter how hard you have worked on it already. Happy people are good at ignoring those sunk costs both when making the decision to walk away from a project and after making the decision to walk away. They don't spend time regretting the "wasted" resources.

Chapter 9:

The Power of Community

The topic that we are going to discuss today is something that I feel has resonated with me one a more personal level recently. And it is one that I have largely neglected in the past.

As i have mentioned before in other videos, that as an entrepreneur of sorts, my job required me to work independently, mostly from home. And while it may sound nice to others, or even yourself, where you think it is a privilege to work from home, many a times it is actually not all that fun because there is no sense of community or interaction with others. And the job becomes quite lonesome.

I'm sure many of you who have experienced lockdowns and Work from home situations, that it may seem fun for a week, but after that you realize that actually it isn't all that it is cracked out to be. And you actually do wanna get dressed, get out of the house, and go somewhere to do your work rather than stay in your PJs all day and waste your time away.

But if you dig deeper, you will realize that what you actually miss is the interaction with your co-workers, to just walk over to their desk to ask them something, or simply to just start a conversation because maybe you're bored, or to have lunch together instead of cooking your own instant noodles at home.

As social creatures, we crave that human interaction. And we crave belonging in a community and being a part of something bigger than ourselves.

When we are in lockdown, we lose that personal touch that we have with others, and we start to feel restless, we feel that something is missing but we can't put our finger on it. It is not the actual work at the job that we look forward to, but rather the people, the colleagues that make working fun and enjoyable.

The same goes for any sports of workout. You will realize that when you gym alone, you are less likely to show up because there is no one there to push you to make you do one more rep. There is no community to keep you going back to stick to your goals. For those of you who do yoga, i am sure the experience is very different when you practice an hour of yoga at home versus in a yoga studio with 30 other people, even if you don't know any of them. There is still a sense that you are a part of a greater unit, a class that works out together, a group of like-minded individuals who really want the same thing and share the same interests. You feel compelled to go back because the community is there to make the exercise fun. That after a tiring workout you look to the people beside and around you and you see the same expressions on their faces. That they had shared an activity with you and feel the same things. Isn't that what life is really about? To be a part of something rather than going about it like a lone wolf?

So for those of you who feel like something is amiss in the activity that you once loved, be it a sports or a job, or an activity that you have no choice to do but never felt happy doing it, i challenge you to find a like-minded community who share the same beliefs and interests. You can easily look for such groups on meet-up apps. You might find that the missing puzzle is indeed other individuals that share your likes. And when you work around them or with them, you will feel a much greater sense of joy and happiness that you never thought you could feel.

I hope you learned something today and I'll see you in the next one. Take care.

How to Eat With Mood in Mind

At the point when you're feeling down, it tends to be enticing to go to food to lift your spirits. Notwithstanding, the sweet, fatty treats that numerous individuals resort to have unfortunate results of their own. Along these lines, you may puzzle over whether any good food sources can work on your temperament.

As of late, research on the connection between sustenance and psychological wellness has been arising. However, note that state of mind can be impacted by numerous variables, like pressure, climate, helpless rest, hereditary qualities, mood disorders, and nutritional deficiencies. In any case, certain food varieties have been displayed to further develop general mental wellbeing and specific kinds of temperament issues.

1. Fatty Fish

Omega-3 unsaturated fats are a gathering of fundamental fats you should get through your eating routine because your body can't produce them all alone. Fatty fish like salmon and tuna fish are wealthy in two sorts of omega-3s — docosahexaenoic corrosive (DHA) and eicosapentaenoic corrosive (EPA) — that are connected to bring down degrees of despair. Omega-3s add to lower your depression and seem to assume key parts in mental health and cell flagging.

2. Dark Chocolate

Chocolate is wealthy in numerous mood-boosting compounds. Its sugar may further develop mood since it's a fast wellspring of fuel for your brain. Besides, it's anything but a course of feel-great mixtures, like caffeine, theobromine, and N-acylethanolamine — a substance synthetically like cannabinoids that have been connected to improved mood.

3. Fermented Food Varieties

Fermented food sources, which incorporate kimchi, yogurt, kefir, fermented tea, and sauerkraut, may further develop gut wellbeing and state of mind. The fermentation interaction permits live microbes to flourish in food varieties ready to change over sugars into liquor and acids. During this interaction, probiotics are made. These live microorganisms support the development of solid microscopic organisms in your gut and may expand serotonin levels.

4. Bananas

Bananas may assist with flipping around a frown.

They're high in nutrient B6, which orchestrates feel-great synapses like dopamine and serotonin.

Moreover, one enormous banana (136 grams) gives 16 grams of sugar and 3.5 grams of fiber.

When matched with fiber, sugar is delivered gradually into your circulation system, considering stable glucose levels and better disposition control. Glucose levels that are too low may prompt irritability and emotional episodes.

5. Oats

Oats are an entire grain that can keep you feeling great the entire morning. You can appreciate them in numerous structures, like, for the time being, oats, oatmeal, muesli, and granola. They're a phenomenal wellspring of fiber, giving 8 grams in a solitary crude cup (81 grams). Fiber eases back your processing of carbs, considering a slow arrival of sugar into the circulation system to keep your energy levels stable.

Chapter 10:

Share Your Wisdom with the World

Today we're going to talk about how to share your wisdom with the world. How many of you think that you have something meaningful to share with others? Whether you are an expert at a particular field, or just that you are particularly good at a certain task.

Have you ever thought about putting your knowledge out there so that people can learn from you?

It is incredibly powerful the gifts that you and I possess. We all have different talents, wisdom, knowledge, that are unique to each individual. No 2 humans are the same, and that goes the same for what they have to offer. What you have to give is uniquely special to you and you only.

I want to bring light to this topic because I too was once afraid to let my voice be heard. I felt that I had no authority, certification, or whatever qualification to be able to write on relationships or about life. I always thought that what I had to say maybe wasn't that important, that it wouldn't help anybody. But i soon realized that it was my own limiting beliefs about myself that were holding me back from sharing my truth with the world.

As I leaned in to more about personal development, I opened my eyes to the wonderful possibilities that we all have to offer as humans. I started to believe that maybe I had something worth sharing. That maybe an article that i wrote or a video that i put out, or an audiobook that i published could help someone somewhere, somehow.

I started to believe that as long as I can change 1 life, that would be good enough a reason for me to spend my time and energy into publishing something that would go out there into the world. Yeah there will be haters. Yes there will be people telling me that what I say is stupid or doesn't make sense, but as long as I believed in what i had to say, it was all that mattered.

We all have a right to share our truth. That truth may not sit well with everyone, but you will find your audience. If you have something to say, put it out there. Help someone in need.

Social media and the internet has become such a powerful force that everything we share can be instantaneously broadcasted all over the world. Think of that kind of power. If you have a powerful voice, a positive one, share it.

that is my challenge for each and everyone of you today. To believe in yourself, your wisdom, and not be afraid to show it to the world.

PART 3

Chapter 1:

<u>The Appetite of Success</u>

What is that you want? What are you hungry for? What eats you up on the inside or sets you on fire? Because that is the measure of your success. Not what other people say, not what career they think you should do, nor how much money they think you should make.

Success is satiating the hunger inside of you.

But the appetite of success cannot be fed once. You don't eat one meal and find yourself full for the rest of your life. That would be crazy. You'd find yourself starved and weak. Delirious. I want to tell you that if you are at a loss, if the world seems to be spinning beyond your control then you are probably starving the appetite of success. Meaning is found in purpose, and purpose is fulfilled through action. SO WHY ARE YOU NOT DOING ANYTHING. If you are feeling empty you are the only one who can choose to fill up again. Find the thing that gets you going and start grinding.

Work has become something negative. We seem to think that work is a burden that we have to bear. But that's not what work was supposed to be, work used to be about finding a craft, a skill that you can hone sharper than the blacksmith's blades next door. It was about turning something interesting into something practical, then turning something practical into something sellable. Nothing has changed! Entrepreneurs still do that, people who enjoy their jobs still do that, YOU can still do that!

But you have to make the choice to chase the thing that challenges you, that calls the craftsman inside of you out. Everyone has the potential to be a master at something, but I feel like a lot of people fail to find their pursuit of mastery. In a noisy world it's hard to hear the call, but if you want to achieve success you have to know what success means to you.

You won't satisfy a craving by having anything else other than what you are craving. Then moment you identify what you are hungry for is the moment you can pursue success, understanding your appetite is the first step to mastery.

So, what are you waiting for!?

Search. Experiment. Pick up new hobbies. I don't care what it takes I care about WHERE IT TAKES YOU. You need to wake up excited and go to sleep satisfied.

Annie Dillard once said that,

"How we spend our days is, of course, how we spend our lives."

If you are just waiting around for something to magically happen, it never will. **Success meets on Mondays and it's time you started showing up**. You should be more concerned with the everyday than the one day. Because one day is just the compound of every day. The only way to change what one day looks like, is to change what today looks like. So, GET GOING!

Chapter 2:

When It Is Time To Let Go and Move On (Career)

Today we're going to talk about a topic that I hope will motivate you to quit that job that you hate or one that you feel that you have nothing more to give anymore.

For the purpose of this video, we will focus mainly on career as I believe many of you may feel as though you are stuck in your job but fear quitting because you are afraid you might not find a better one.

For today's topic, I want to draw attention to a close friend of mine who have had this dilemma for years and still hasn't decided to quit because he is afraid that he might not get hired by someone else.

In the beginning of my friend's career, he was full of excitement in his new job and wanted to do things perfectly. Things went pretty smoothly over the course of the first 2 years, learning new things, meeting new friends, and getting settled into his job that he thought he might stay on for a long time to come seeing that it was the degree that he had pursued in university. However when the 3rd year came along, he started to feel jaded with his job. Everyday he would meet ungrateful and sometimes mean customers who were incredibly self-entitled. They would be rude and he started dreading going to work more and more each day. This aspect of the job wore him down and he started to realise that he wasn't happy at all with his work.

Having had a passion for fitness for a while now, he realized that he felt very alive when he attended fitness classes and enjoyed working out and teaching others how to work out. He would fiddle with the idea of attending a teacher training course that would allow him to be a professional and certified fitness coach.

As his full time job started to become more of a burden, he became more serious about the prospect of switching careers and pursuing a new one entirely. At his job, realized that the company wasn't generous at all with the incentives and gruelling work hours, but he stayed on as he was afraid he wouldn't find another job in this bad economy. The fear was indeed real so he kept delaying trying to quit his job. Before he knew it 3 years more had passed and by this time he full on dreaded every single minute at his job.

It was not until he made that faithful decision one day to send in his resignation letter and to simultaneously pay for the teacher training course to become a fitness instructor did his fortunes start to change for him. The fortunes in this wasn't about money. It was about freedom. It was about growth. And it was about living.

We all know deep in our hearts when it is time to call it quits to something. When we know that there is nothing more that we can possibly give to our job. That no amount of time more could ever fulfill that void in us. That we just simply need to get out and do something different.

You see, life is about change. As we grow, our priorities change, our personalities change, our expectations change, and our passions and our interests change as well. If we stay in one place too long, especially in a field or in something that we have hit a wall at, we will feel stuck, and we will feel dread. We will feel that our time spent is not productive and we end up feeling hopeless and sorry for ourselves.

Instead when we choose to let go, when we choose to call time on something, we open up the doors for time on other ventures, and other adventures. And our world becomes brighter again.

I challenge each and everyone of you to take a leap of faith. You know deep in your hearts when it is time to move on from your current job and find the next thing. If you dont feel like you are growing, or if you feel that you absolutely hate your job because there is no ounce of joy that you can derive from it, move on immediately. Life is too short to be spending 10 hours of your life a day on something that you hate, that sucks the living soul out of you. Give yourself the time and space to explore, to find some other path for you to take. You will be surprised what might happen when you follow your heart.

I hope you learned something today, take care and I'll see you in the next one.

Chapter 3:

Happy People Only Focus on What Is Within Their Control

We cloud our judgment and lose the sense of our role in shaping our reality.

Such can be the case today.

We're fighting through a global pandemic, and I can assure you every one of us is having good days and bad days.

On the good days, we try to stay positive and be productive. On the bad days, we sulk into the worry of predicting what the future will be like. We imagine it, and then we start living it, which leaves us feeling helpless and scared.

Thoughts fire before emotions—that's why when we think negatively, we feel negative emotions.

But there's a way around this.

Whenever I find myself moving from a positive outlook to a negative one, I try my best to bring my attention back to the most important aspect of all.

I ask myself these three questions:

1. What is worrying me?

2. What is within my control?

3. What matters most to me, and what can I do about it?

When we focus on what we can control, our thoughts empower us and then trigger positive emotions.

Do we give our power away to factors we cannot control, or do we retain it and direct our energy onto the options we can control?

When my mind plays tricks on me and slides me into a stream of worry, I consciously try to swim out of it. And I use this framework below to reorient my thoughts and whisk them up into a more sunny state of mind.

A Sunshine State of Mind

At any given stage in your life, regardless of the set of circumstances you are dealing with, you can find yourself in one of four mental states:

- **Quadrant #1: Wasting your energy.** When you focus on what is not within your control, you're wasting your energy on factors that will not move you forward. This is like having a 2-week vacation booked, which was canceled due to the pandemic. You can complain all you want, but what's the use? Stop draining your energy on it and start thinking clearly.

- **Quadrant #2: Being paranoid.** When you ignore what is not within your control, you're paranoid. You shouldn't ignore external factors, instead, accept what is and be aware of the external conditions that are outside your control. For instance, with this pandemic, we must understand the situation and how it progresses because its advancements have implications on our lives. We don't want to give our undivided attention, but we do want to stay educated on it.

- **Quadrant #3: In a sunshine state of mind.** When you focus on what is within your control, you're in the driver's seat. You're intentional about your attitude and how you spend your energy. This is where you are emotionally mature and thinking rationally and clearly in a sunshine state of mind. And what does it do to you? It keeps you positive, energized, and motivated.

Chapter 4:

How To Find Your Passion

Today we're going to talk about a topic that i think many of you are interested to know about. And that is how to find your passion.

For many of us, the realities of work and obligations means that we end up doing something we dislike for the money in the hopes that it might buy us some happiness. That sometimes we stop following our passion because maybe it does not exactly pay very well. And that is a fair decision to make.

But today, i hope to be able to help you follow at least one passion project at any point in your life in the hopes that it might help elevate your spirits, give your life more meaning, and help you live each day with a renewed drive and purpose.

You see, the world can be very dull if we chase something that we actually don't really feel attracted to. For example, when we are forced to do something out of sheer dread day in and day out, it will suck the living soul out of us and we will tend to fall into the trap of running an endless wheel with no hope in sight. When we chase material things for example, money or luxury products, we sell our soul to a job that pays well physically but not emotionally and spiritually. As a human being, we have traded our very essence and time, for a piece of paper or digital currency that serves no purpose than to enrich us externally. While it might feel good to be living comfortably, past a certain threshold, there is a point of diminishing returns. And more money just doesn't bring you that much joy anymore.

Yes you may have the fanciest, car, house, and whatever physical possessions you have. But how many of you have heard stories of people who have a lot of money but end up depressed, or end up blowing it all away because they can never spend enough to satisfy their cravings for physical goods and services. What these people lacked in emotional growth, they tried to overcompensate with money. And as their inner self gets emptier and emptier, they themselves get poorer and poorer as well.

On the flip side, many would argue that passion is overrated. That passion is nothing but some imaginary thing that we tell ourselves we need to have in order to be happy. But i am here to argue that you do not need to make passion your career in order to be happy.

You see, passion is an aspiration, passion is something that excites you, passion is something that you would do even if it does not pay a single cent. That you would gladly trade your time readily for even if it meant u weren't getting anything monetary in return. Because this passion unlocks something within you that cannot be explained with being awarded physical prizes. It is the feeling that you are truly alive and happy, you are so incredibly grateful and thankful to be doing at that very moment in time, that nothing else mattered, not even sleep.

To me, and I hope you will see this too, that passion can be anything you make it out to be. It can be something as simple as a passion for singing, a passion for creating music, a passion for helping others, passion for supporting your family, passion for starting a family, passion for doing charity work, passion for supporting a cause monetarily, or even a passion for living life to the fullest and being grateful each day.

For some lucky ones, they have managed to marry their passion with their career. They have somehow made their favourite thing to do their job, and it fulfills them each day. To those people, i congratulate you and envy you.

But for the rest of us, our passion can be something we align our soul with as long as it fulfils us as well. If we have multiple mouths to feed, we can make our passion as being the breadwinner to provide for our family if it brings us joy to see them happy. If we have a day job that we hate but can't let go off for whatever reasons, we can have a passion for helping others, to use the income that we make to better the lives of others.

And for those who have free time but are not sure what to do with it, to just simply start exploring different interests and see what hobbies you resonate with. You may never know what you might discover if you did a little digging.

What I have come to realize is that passions rarely stay the same. They change as we change, they evolve over time just as we grow. And many of the passions we had when we were younger, we might outgrow them when we hit a certain age. As our priorities in life change, our passions follow along.

In my opinion, you do not need to make your passion your career in order to be truly happy.. I believe that all you need is to have at least 1 passion project at any given point of time in your life to sustain you emotionally and spiritually. Something that you can look forward to on your off days, in your time away from work, that you can pour all your time and energy into willingly without feeling that you have wasted any second. And who knows, you might feel so strongly about that passion project that you might even decide to make it your career some day. The thing is you never really know. Life is mysterious like that.

All I do know is that chasing money for the wrong reasons will never net u happiness. But having a passion, whatever it may be, will keep you grounded and alive.

So I challenge each and everyone of you today to look into your current life, and see there are any bright spots that you have neglected that you could revive and make it your passion project. Remember that passion can be anything you make out to be as long as you derive fulfilment and happiness from it. Helpfully one that isnt material or monetary.

Chapter 5:

Twenty Percent of Effort Produces 80% of Results

Today we're going to talk about the 80-20 rule and how you can apply it to your life for great results in whatever you are doing. For the purposes of this video we are going to use income as a measurement of success. This will directly translate to productivity and the areas that you are spending your most time and energy.

Have you ever wondered why no matter how much time you end up working, that your paycheck never seems to rise? That your income and finance seems to be stagnant? Or have you ever wondered, for those of you who have ventured into creating a second or third stream of income on the side, that you might actually spend lesser on those activities and earn a bigger income in proportion to the time you actually spent to run those side businesses?

This is where the 80-20 rule comes into play. For those that have not seen their bank account or income grow despite the immense amount of effort put it, It may be that 80% of time you are spending it doing things that actually have little or no change to the growth of your networth. The work simply isn't actually worth 80% of your attention.

Rather you may want to look elsewhere, to that 20%, if you want to see real change. I would recommend that instead of banging your head against the wall at your day job, try looking for something to do on the side. It may be just your passion, or it may be something you foresee greater potential returns. Start taking action on those things. It could be the very thing that you were searching for this whole time. If the rule applies, you should be spending majority of your time and energy into this 20%. By focusing on the tasks that has the greatest rewards, you are working smart instead of working hard now. Only when you can identify what exactly those tasks are can you double down on them for great success.

There were times in my life that I spent a lot of my time trying to force something to work. But no matter how hard I tried, I just couldn't see a breakthrough. It was only after further exploration through trials and errors did I finally come up with a set list of tasks that I knew were profitable. That if I kept doing them over and over again I would be able to grow my wealth consistently. By spending all of my time doing these specific tasks, I was able to eliminate all the noise and to focus my actions to a narrow few. And I was surprised at the outsized rewards it brought me.

If you know that something isn't working, don't be afraid to keep looking, trying, and exploring other ways. Keep a close tab on the time you spend in these areas and the income that flows in. Only when you measure everything can you really know where you are going wrong and where you are going right.

Remember that 20% of the effort produces 80% of the results. So I challenge all of you to stop spending 80% of the effort doing things that only produce 20% of the results. It is better to work smart than to work hard. Trust me. I believe that you will be able to find what those things are if you put your mind to it.

I hope you learned something today, take care and I'll see you in the next one.

The Lure of Wanting Luxury Items

Have you ever walked by a store and pondered over those LV bags if you were a lady? Secretly hoping that you can get your hands on one of those bags so that you can feel good about yourself when you carry them on your shoulders? Or have you ever glanced at a boutique watch shop if you were a guy hoping that you can get your hands on one of the rolexes which costs north of $10k minimum? That could be the same lust and desire for the latest and greatest cars, apple products, clothing, etc. anything you name it.

You think of saving up a year's worth of salary just to be able to afford one of these things and you see yourself feeling good about it and that you can brag to your friends and show off to people that you have the latest and most expensive product on the market. and you imagine yourself being happy that it is all you will need to stay happy.

I am here to tell you that the lure of owning luxury items can only make you happy to a certain extent. And only if purchasing these things is something of great meaning to you, like achieving a big milestone that you want to commemorate in life. In that instance, walking into that store to purchase that luxury product can be a great experience and of great significance as well. Whether it be a birthday gift to yourself, or commemorating a wedding anniversary, job/career work milestone, or any of that in nature, you will tend to hold these products with great sentimental value and hardly will you ever sell these items should the opportunity arise to make a profit from them (which is generally not the case with most things you buy).

I will argue that when you pick these products to wear from your wardrobe, you will indeed be filled with feelings of happiness, but it is not the product itself that makes you happy, but it is the story behind it, the hard work, the commemorative occasion that you will associate and remember these products for. It will transport you back in time to that place in your life when you made the purchase and you will indeed relive that emotion that took you there to the store in the first place. That to me is a meaningful luxury purchase that is not based on lust or greed, but of great significance.

But what if you are just someone who is chasing these luxury products just because everyone else has it? When you walk down the street and you see all these people carrying these products and you just tell yourself you have to have it or else? You find all the money you can dig from your savings and emergency fund to pay for that product? I would argue that in that instance, you will not be as happy as you thought you would be. These kinds of wants just simply do not carry the weight of any importance. And after feeling good for a few days after you owned that luxury good, you feel a deep sense of emptiness because it really does not make you a happier person. Instead you are someone trying to have something but with that comes a big hole in your wallet or your bank account. The enthusiasm and excitement starts to fade away and you wonder whats the next luxury good you need to buy to feel that joy again.

You see, material goods cannot fill us with love and happiness. Luxury goods are only there to serve one purpose, to reward you for your hard work and that you can comfortably purchase it without regret and worry that you are left financially in trouble. The lure of many of us is that we tend to want what we can't have. It could also turn into an obsession for many of us where we just keep buying more and more of these luxury goods to satisfy our craving for materialistic things. You will realise one day that the pursuit never ends, the more you see, the more you want. And that is just how our brains are wired.

I have a confession to make, I had an obsession for apple products myself and I always thought I wanted the latest and greatest apple products every year when a new model comes out. And every year apple seems to know how to satisfy my lust for these products and manages to make me spend thousands of dollars every time they launch something new. This addiction i would say lasted for a good 8 years until I recently realised that the excitement ALWAYS fades after a week or two. Sure it is exciting to play with it for a couple of days while your brain gets used to this incredible piece of technology sitting in front of you. But after a week or two, I am left wondering, whats next? I began to realise that what really made me happy was doing what i love, engaging in my favourite hobbies, meeting friends, and just living simply without so many wants in life. When you have less wants, you automatically go into a mindset of abundance. And that is a great feeling to have.

I challenge all of you today to question what is your real motivation behind wanted to buy luxury items. Is it to commemorate a significant achievement in your life? or is it a meaningless lust for something that you want to emulate others for. Dig deeper and you will find the answer. Thank you

Chapter 6:

The 5 Second Rule

Today I'm going to share with you a very special rule in life that has worked wonders for me ever since I discovered it. And that is known as the 5 second rule by Mel Robbins.

You see, on a daily basis, I struggle with motivation and getting things done. I struggle with the littlest things like replying an email, to responding to a work request. This struggle has become such a bad habit that before I think about beginning any sort of work, I would first turn on my Netflix account to watch an episode or two of my favourite sitcom, telling myself that I will get right on it after I satisfy this side of me first.

This habit of procrastination soon became so severe that I would actually sit and end up wasting 4-5 hours of time every morning before I would actually even begin on any work-related stuff. Before I knew it, it would be 3pm and I haven't gotten a single thing done. All the while I was staring at the clock, counting the number of hours I have wasted, while simultaneously addicted to procrastinating that I just could not for the life of me get myself off the couch onto my desk to begin any meaningful work.

I realized that something had to change. If I kept this up, I would not only not get anything done, like ever, but i would also begin to loathe myself for being so incredibly unproductive and useless. This process of self-loathing got worse everyday I leaned into the habit of procrastination. It was only until i stumbled onto Mel Robbin's 5 second rule that I started to see a real change in my habits.

The rule is simple, to count backwards from 5 and to just get up and go do that thing. It sounded stupid to me at first, but it worked. Instead of laying around in bed every morning checking my phone before I woke up, I would count backwards from 5 and as soon as it hit 1, i would get up and head straight towards the shower, or I would pack up my things and get out of my house.

I had identified that staying at home was the one factor that made me the most unproductive person on the planet, and that the only way I knew I was going to get real work done, was to get out of the house. I had also identified that showering was a good way to cleanse my mind from the night before. I really enjoyed showering as I always seem to have a clear head afterwards to be able to focus. What works for me, may not necessarily work for you. You have to identify for yourself when are the times you are most productive, and simply replicate it. A good way to find out is by journaling, which I will talk about in a separate video. Journaling is a good way to capture a moment in time and a particular state of mind. Try it for yourself the next time you are incredibly focused, write down how you got to that state, and simply do it again the next time to get there.

The 5 second rule is so simple yet so powerful because it snaps our unhealthy thought patterns. As Mel puts it, our brain is hardwired to protect us. We procrastinate out of fear of doing the things that are hard, so we have to beat our brain to it by disrupting it first. When we decide to move and take action after reaching 1, it is too late for our brains to stop us. And we get the ball rolling.

I was at my most productive on days that I felt my worst. But I overcame it because I didn't let my brain stop me from myself. I wouldn't say that I am struggle free now, but i knew i had a tool that would work most of the time to get me out of procrastination and into doing some serious work that would move my life forward. There are times when I would forget about the 5 second rule and my bad habits would kick in, but I always reminded myself that it was available to me if I chose to use it.

I would urge all of you who are struggling with any form of procrastination or laziness to give the 5 second rule a try. All you need to do is to get started and the rest becomes easy.

Happy People Find Reasons to Laugh and Forge Deep Connections

"…Making a connection with men and women through humour, happiness and laughter not only helps you make new friends, but it is the means to establish a strong, meaningful connection to people."

People always try to have a personality that attracts people and makes them feel comfortable around them. Utilizing their humour has been one of those ways to create new friendships. But once you start doing this, you will realize that this humorous nature has emotions and attitudes that comprise happiness and positivity. This will also help you create deep and meaningful connections that will last a lifetime.

When you intend to focus on humour to find deep connections, your subconscious mind starts focusing on positivity. You will slowly turn out to be more positive in your reasoning and conduct because awareness of what's funny is truly only demonstrative of one's very own bliss. In this manner, you're sustaining a more appealing, and that's just the beginning "contagious" attitude. Similarly, as we search out bliss in our everyday lives through satisfying work, leisure activities, individual interests and day to day life, so too do people seek out and wish to be encircled by joy on a relational level: joy and bitterness are contagious, and we as a whole wish to get the happy bug.

Humour helps fashion friendships since we wish to encircle ourselves with individuals who are glad. This way, our objective shouldn't just be to utilize humour to make new companions, however to zero in on the entirety of the uplifting perspectives and feelings that include an entertaining and carefree nature. By embodying satisfaction, inspiration, happiness, receptiveness and tranquillity, we sustain a more grounded and "contagious" state of being.

Historically there was a negative connotation attached to humour, but over the years, research was done, and it proved otherwise. In any case, research on humour has come into the daylight, with humour currently seen as a character strength. Good brain science, a field that analyzes what individuals progress admirably, notes that humour can be utilized to cause others to feel better, acquire closeness, or help buffer pressure. Alongside appreciation, expectation and otherworldliness, a funny bone has a place with the arrangement of qualities positive clinicians call greatness; together, they help us manufacture associations with the world and give significance to life. Enthusiasm for humour corresponds with different qualities, as well, like insight and love of learning. Furthermore, humour exercises or activities bring about expanded sensations of passionate prosperity and idealism.

Once you step into adulthood, it can be difficult for many people to form friendships and then keep up with them because all of us get busier in our lives. Still, it's never too much to go to a bar and strike up a conversation with a random person and believe us, if you have a good sense of humour, they will be naturally attracted towards you.

Chapter 7:

The Difference Between Professionals and Amateurs

It doesn't matter what you are trying to become better at. If you only do the work when you're motivated, then you'll never be consistent enough to become a professional. The ability to show up every day, stick to the schedule, and do the work, especially when you don't feel like it — is so valuable that you need to become better 99% of the time. I've seen this in my own experiences. When I don't miss workouts, I get in the best shape of my life. When I write every week, I become a better writer. When I travel and take my camera out every day, I take better photos. It's simple and powerful. But why is it so difficult?

The Pain of Being A Pro

Approaching your goals — whatever they are — with the attitude of a professional isn't easy. Being a pro is painful. The simple fact of the matter is that most of the time, we are inconsistent. We all have goals that we would like to achieve and dreams that we would like to fulfill, but it doesn't matter what you are trying to become better at. If you only do the work when it's convenient or exciting, then you'll never be consistent enough to achieve remarkable results.

I can guarantee that if you manage to start a habit and keep sticking to it, there will be days when you feel like quitting. When you start a business, there will be days when you don't feel like showing up. When you're at the gym, there will be sets that you don't feel like finishing. When it's time to write, there will be days that you don't feel like typing. But stepping up when it's annoying or painful or draining to do so, that's what makes the difference between a professional and an amateur.

Professionals stick to the schedule. Amateurs let life get in the way. Professionals know what is important to them and work towards it with purpose. Amateurs get pulled off course by the urgencies of life. **You'll Never Regret Starting Important Work.**

Some people might think I'm promoting the benefits of being a workaholic. "Professionals work harder than everyone else, and that's why they're great." That's not it at all.

Being a pro is about having the discipline to commit to what is important to you instead of merely saying something is important to you. It's about starting when you feel like stopping, not because you want to work more, but because your goal is important enough to you that you don't simply work on it when it's convenient. Becoming a pro is about making your priorities a reality.

There have been many sets that I haven't felt like finishing, but I've never regretted doing the workout. There have been many articles I haven't felt like writing, but I've never regretted publishing on schedule. There have been many days I've felt like relaxing, but I've never regretted showing up and working on something important to me.

Becoming a pro doesn't mean you're a workaholic. It means that you're good at making time for what matters to you — especially when you don't feel like it — instead of playing the role of the victim and letting life happen to you.

7 Ways To Cultivate Emotions That Will Lead You To Greatness

Billions of men and women have walked the earth but only a handful have made their names engraved in history forever. These handful of people have achieved 'greatness' owing to their outstanding work, their passion and their character.

Now, greatness doesn't come overnight—greatness is not something you can just reach out and grab. Greatness is the result of how you have lived your entire life and what you have achieved in your lifetime. Against all your given circumstances, how impactful your life has been in this world, how much value you have given to the people around you, how much difference your presence has made in history counts towards how great you are. However, even though human greatness is subjective, people who are different and who have stood out from everyone else in a particular matter are perceived as great.

However, cultivating greatness in life asks for a 'great' deal of effort and all kinds of human effort are influenced by human emotions. So it's safe to say that greatness is, in fact, controlled by our emotions. Having said that, let's see what emotions are associated with greatness and how to cultivate them in real life:

1.   Foster Gratitude

You cannot commence your journey towards greatness without being grateful first. That's right, being satisfied with what you already have in life and expressing due gratitude towards it will be your first step towards greatness. Being in a gratified emotional state at most times (if not all) will enhance your mental stability which will consequently help you perceive life in a different—or better point of view. This enhanced perception of life will remove your stresses and allow you to develop beyond the mediocrity of life and towards greatness.

2. Be As Curious As Child

Childhood is the time when a person starts to learn whatever that is around them. A child never stops questioning, a child never runs away from what they have to face. They just deal with things head on. Such kind of eagerness for life is something that most of us lose at the expense of time. As we grow up—as we know more, our interest keeps diminishing. We stop questioning anymore and accept what is. Eventually, we become entrapped into the ordinary. On the contrary, if we greet everything in life with bold eagerness, we expose ourselves to opportunities. And opportunities lead to greatness.

3. Ignite Your Passion

Passion has become a cliché term in any discussion related to achievements and life. Nevertheless, there is no way of denying the role of passion in driving your life force. Your ultimate zeal and fervor towards what you want in life is what distinguishes you to be great.

Because admittedly, many people may want the same thing in life but how bad they want it—the intensity of wanting something is what drives people to stand out from the rest and win it over.

4. Become As Persistent As A Mountain

There are two types of great people on earth—1) Those who are born great and 2) Those who persistently work hard to become great. If you're reading this article, you probably belong to the later criteria. Being such, your determination is a key factor towards becoming great. Let nothing obstruct you—remain as firm as a mountain through all thick and thin. That kind of determination is what makes extraordinary out of the ordinary.

5. Develop Adaptability

As I have mentioned earlier, unless you are born great, your journey towards greatness will be an extremely demanding one. You will have to embrace great lengths beyond your comfort. In order to come out successful in such a journey, make sure that you become flexible to unexpected changes in your surroundings. Again, making yourself adaptable first in another journey in itself. You can't make yourself fit in adverse situations immediately. Adaptability or flexibility is cultivated prudently, with time, exposing yourself to adversities, little by little.

6. Confidence Is Key

Road to greatness often means that you have to tread a path that is discouraged by most. It's obvious—by definition, everybody cannot be great. People will most likely advise against you when you aspire something out of the ordinary. Some will even present logical explanations against you;especially your close ones. But nothing should waver your faith. You must remain boldly confident towards what you're pursuing. Only you can bring your greatness. Believe that.

7. Sense of Fulfilment Through Contributions

Honestly, there can be no greater feeling than what you'd feel after your presence has made a real impact on this world. If not, what else do we live for? Having contributed to the world and the people around you; this is the purpose of life. All the big and small contributions you make give meaning to your existence. It connects you to others, man and animal alike. It fulfills your purpose as a human being. We live for this sense of fulfillment and so, become a serial contributor. Create in yourself a greed for this feeling. At the end of the day, those who benefit from your contributions will revere you as great. No amount of success can be compared with this kind of greatness. So, never miss the opportunity of doing a good deed, no matter how minuscule or enormous.

In conclusion, these emotions don't come spontaneously. You have to create these emotions, cultivate them. And to cultivate these emotions, you must first understand yourself and your goals. With your eye on the prize, you have to create these emotions in you which will pave the path to your greatness. Gratitude, curiosity, passion, persistence, adaptability and fulfillment—each has its own weight and with all the emotions at play, nothing can stop you from becoming great in the truest form.

Chapter 8:

Enjoying The Simple Things

Today we're going to talk about a topic that might sound cheesy, but trust me it's worth taking a closer look at. And that is how we should strive to enjoy the simple things in life.

Many of us think we need a jam packed schedule for the week, month, or year, to tell us that we are leading a very productive and purposeful life. We find ways to fill our time with a hundred different activities. Going to this event, that event, never slowing down. And we find ourselves maybe slightly burnt out by the end of it.

We forget that sometimes simplicity is better than complication. Have you sat down with your family for a simple lunch meal lately? You don't have to talk, you just have to be in each other's company and enjoying the food that is being served in front of you.

I found myself appreciating these moments more than I did running around to activities thinking that I needed something big to be worth my time. I found sitting next to my family on the couch watching my own shows while they watch theirs very rewarding. I found eating alone at my favourite restaurant while watching my favourite sitcom to be equally as enjoyable as hanging out with a group of 10 friends. I also found myself richly enjoying a long warm shower every morning and evening. It is the highlights of my day.

My point is that we need to start looking at the small things we can do each day that will bring us joy. Things that are within our control. Things that we know can hardly go wrong. This will provide some stability to gain some pleasure from. The little nuggets in the day that will not be determined by external factors such as the weather, friends bailing on us, or irritating customers.

When we focus on the little things, we make life that much better to live through.

8 Ways To Love Yourself First

"Your task is not to seek for love, but merely to seek and find all the barriers within yourself that you have built against it." - Rumi.

Most of us are so busy waiting for someone to come into our lives and love us that we have forgotten about the one person we need to love the most – ourselves. Most psychologists agree that being loved and being able to love is crucial to our happiness. As quoted by Sigmund Freud, "love and work ... work and love. That's all there is." It is the mere relationship of us with ourselves that sets the foundation for all other relationships and reveals if we will have a healthy relationship or a toxic one.

Here are some tips on loving yourself first before searching for any kind of love in your life.

1. Know That Self-Love Is Beautiful

Don't ever consider self-love as being narcissistic or selfish, and these are two completely different things. Self-love is rather having positive regard for our wellbeing and happiness. When we adopt self-love, we see higher levels of self-esteem within ourselves, are less critical and harsh with ourselves while making mistakes, and can celebrate our positive qualities and accept all our negative ones.

2. Always be kind to yourself:

We are humans, and humans are tended to get subjected to hurts, shortcomings, and emotional pain. Even if our family, friends, or even our partners may berate us about our inadequacies, we must learn to accept ourselves with all our imperfections and flaws. We look for acceptance from others and be harsh on ourselves if they tend to be cruel or heartless with us. We should always focus on our many positive qualities, strengths, and abilities, and admirable traits; rather than harsh judgments, comparisons, and self-hatred get to us. Always be gentle with yourself.

3.   Be the love you feel within yourself:

You may experience both self-love and self-hatred over time. But it would be best if you always tried to focus on self-love more. Try loving yourself and having positive affirmations. Do a love-kindness meditation or spiritual practices to nourish your soul, and it will help you feel love and compassion toward yourself. Try to be in that place of love throughout your day and infuse this love with whatever interaction you have with others.

4.   Give yourself a break:

We don't constantly live in a good phase. No one is perfect, including ourselves. It's okay to not be at the top of your game every day, or be happy all the time, or love yourself always, or live without pain. Excuse your bad days and embrace all your imperfections and mistakes. Accept your negative emotions but don't let them overwhelm you. Don't set high standards for yourself, both emotionally and mentally. Don't judge yourself for whatever you feel, and always embrace your emotions wholeheartedly.

5. Embrace yourself:

Are you content to sit all alone because the feelings of anxiety, fear, guilt, or judgment will overwhelm you? Then you have to practice being comfortable in your skin. Go within and seek solace in yourself, practice moments of alone time and observe how you treat yourself. Allow yourself to be mindful of your beliefs, feelings, and thoughts, and embrace solitude. The process of loving yourself starts with understanding your true nature.

6. Be grateful:

Rhonda Bryne, the author of The Magic, advises, "When you are grateful for the things you have, no matter how small they may be, you will see those things instantly increase." Look around you and see all the things that you are blessed to have. Practice gratitude daily and be thankful for all the things, no matter how good or bad they are. You will immediately start loving yourself once you realize how much you have to be grateful for.

7. Be helpful to those around you:

You open the door for divine love the moment you decide to be kind and compassionate toward others. "I slept and dreamt that life was a joy. I awoke and saw that life was service. I acted, and behold, and service was a joy." - Rabindranath Tagore. The love and positive vibes that you wish upon others and send out to others will always find a way back to you. Your soul tends to rejoice when you are kind, considerate, and compassionate. You have achieved the highest form of self-love when you decide to serve others. By helping others, you will realize that you don't need someone else to feel complete; you are complete. It will help you feel more love and fulfillment in your life.

8. Do things you enjoy doing:

If you find yourself stuck in a monotonous loop, try to get some time out for yourself and do the things that you love. There must be a lot of hobbies and passions that you might have put a brake on. Dust them off and start doing them again. Whether it's playing any sport, learning a new skill, reading a new book, writing in on your journal, or simply cooking or baking for yourself, start doing it again. We shouldn't compromise on the things that make us feel alive. Doing the things we enjoy always makes us feel better about ourselves and boost our confidence.

Conclusion:

Loving yourself is nothing short of a challenge. It is crucial for your emotional health and ability to reach your best potential. But the good news is, we all have it within us to believe in ourselves and live the best life we possibly can. Find what you are passionate about, appreciate yourself, and be grateful for what's in your life. Accept yourself as it is.

Chapter 9:

The Magic of the 5 Minute Rule

Recently I have been struggling to get things done, more so than usual. It has become a daily battle with myself to sit down on my desk to begin the necessary work that I know i need to do. However looking at the endless list of tasks i have in front of me, i can't help but to choose procrastination and slacking over beginning my work. And it has affected my ability to be a productive member of society.

Whilst I knew in the back of my mind that I believe the work that I do can benefit society, and that it has the power to give me freedom of time and money to get and do the things that i really wanted to do in life, on some level it wasn't actually enough to get me to start the work. Many a times I felt really sluggish and it would take some strong reminders to get me motivated enough to start the work. That was the point where i decided i needed to search for a solution that work not only make work more enjoyable, but to also push me to get work started much faster without delay.

After spending some solid hours researching, i came across one strategy that I felt would work like a charm on me. And that is to employ the 5 minute rule to every single task that I have on hand.

The biggest problem that I have currently is that I am working on 10 different projects at any one time. And when I look at these 10 separate projects that need my attention, I can't help but feel overwhelmed about the number of hours that I needed to schedule for each of these projects. And that seemed like a mountainous task for me to climb. And looking at it as a whole, it felt absolutely daunting and impossible. Which was what made me not want to even attempt to begin that climb.

How the 5 minute rule works is that for every project that I needed to work on, I wrote that I only needed to do the task for 5 minutes. However ridiculous that sounded, it actually worked like a charm. My brain was tricked into thinking that this became much more manageable and i would accomplish it easily. And we all know that the biggest problem is getting started. But once u do, you tend to keep going. And so for every task that i told myself i needed to do for 5 minutes, in reality i ended up spending the adequate amount of time i needed to do to get the job done. whether it be 10 minutes, 30minutes, an hour, or even several hours.

I managed to trick my brain into breaking each project down to its most basic manageable form and that gave me to confidence that I could crush it with ease. I applied this technique to not only work, but also going to the gym, walking my dog, and other administrative and personal tasks that I was lazy to do. And i saw my ability to begin each task and eventually check it off my to-do list increase exponentially. My productivity level also skyrocketed as a result.

With this simple trick in your arsenal. I believe anyone that you too can begin your work much quicker as well and crush every single task that will be put in front of you today and in your future. So i challenge each and everyone of you today to just tell yourself that you will only need to set aside 5 mins for each task and see where that takes you, and that I believe will be in the right direction.

10 Habits of Taylor Swift

Well-versed pop star isn't the only description for the "American Sweetheart" Taylor Swift- She's a woman with many talents and abilities. As a world-famous singer-songwriter, accomplished businesswoman, and fitness guru, Swift has risen to become one of the world's most renowned celebrities.

She signed her first record deal at the age of 15, has been nominated for over 500 awards, has won 324, and has sold over 50 million albums. Such success did not simply land to her automatically. As per the new Netflix documentary Miss Americana, Swift's growth is a journey of countless disappointing and challenging life and career lessons.

Here are 10 habits of Taylor Swift that can enrich your life and career path.

1. Certainty

Getting to where you want to be in life credits a clear vision. With a sense of clarity, you can pave the way to reach that destination.

Since the day she started her career in music, Taylor Swift has been clear on what she wanted. From the very young age she has served to steer her decision making, and enjoyed every bit of it.

2. Focus on the Brighter Side

Taylor Swift has had a share of public scandals, tabloids exploitation, and people who aimed at tarnishing her name with controversy. It is irrelevant whether they are justified or not, she continues to produce and thrive in her positive space. Just like Taylor Swift, develop an urge to always working past the ruins while strengthening your optimistic moods.

3. You Have No Control Over What Happens

The incident at 2009 VMAs with Kanye West fuelled Swift's desire to prove that her talent is undeniable. You'll learn from the Concert's footage performing her most critically acclaimed song, "All Too Well", that she's was not up to changing what people would eventually say about her but was only concerned with respecting her work ethic. Make your response to criticism a reflection of respect for your hustle!

4. Credit Your Success to Having a Niche

In the entertainment business, and with successful people like Taylor Swift, each one has their unique niche/speciality that sets them apart from everyone else. Major deeply on what makes you unique and what brought you there as your storyline is only for you to tell.

5. Courage Is the Secret to Longevity

Taylor went from being a trial for sexual assault, which she won the case, to her mother ailing from breast cancer and brain tumour to all the publicized stunts she had been through. Despite the challenges, she managed to produce indisputably remarkable projects. Just like Taylor, your confidence, resilience, brilliance, work ethic, and steadfast trust in your process will definitely garner appreciation and respect.

6. Own Your Power

Taylor Swift not only has power, but she also owns it. Following Scooter Braun and Scott Borchetta incident, Taylor was not scared to jeopardize her image or face the consequences of speaking up against something she honestly believed was unfair.

There are always risks to speaking out, but sitting silence may be far riskier. In some circumstances, being silent may endanger your opportunity to manage a project or receive a promotion or increase.

7. Develop Your Support System

Nurture your relationships if you'd like to gain more influence. Even though you are not on the same scale as Taylor Swift, maintained friendships influences your world. Listen to them if you want them to listen to you.

8. Follow Your Heroes

Taylor Swift started her profession at a young age. Her childhood was fraught with difficulties but had motivation from her idols, whom she followed their advice. If you adore someone who influences your life path, emulating two or three things from them pays off.

9. Be Influential

Taylor's success in the music industry has been her driving force in influencing other people. You don't have to have her numbers to be impactful. When you devote your time and energy to becoming productive, influential stats and metrics will follow you.

10. Maintain a Healthy Lifestyle

Being a celebrity doesn't mean that Swift's healthy lifestyle is about trendy diets and strange eating habits that dominates the entire Hollywood culture. According to PopSugar, Swift eats salads, nutritious sandwiches, yoghurt and hit the gym regularly during the week.

Conclusion

You don't have to be Taylor Swift, but you can learn from her. Increase your influence, cultivate your network, develop credibility, wield your authority, focus on positivity, resilience is vital, and feel free to stand your ground as you work on your uniqueness.

Chapter 10:

If Today Was Your Last Day

If today was your last day, what would you do with your life? Steve Jobs once said that "For the past 33 years, I have looked in trhe mirror every morning and asked myself: **'If today** were the **last day** of my life, would I want to do what I am about to do **today**? ' And whenever the answer has been 'No' for too many **days** in a row, I know I need to change something.".

Do you agree with that statement? For me I believe that it is true to a certain extent. I argue that not many of us have the luxury of doing what we love to do every single day. As much as we want to work at that dream job or earn that great salary, or whatever that ideal may be, for some of us who have to feed a family or make ends meet, it is just not possible. And we choose to make that sacrifice to work at a job that we may not like, or go through a routine that sometimes might seem a drag. But that's a personal choice that we choose to make and that is okay too.

On the flip side, i do believe that for those who have the luxury and the choice to pursue whatever careers, dreams, hobbies, and interests we want to pursue, that we should go for it and not live life in regret. I have heard of countless friends who work at a job they hate day in and day out, complaining about their life every single day and about how miserable they are, but are too afraid to leave that job in fear of not being able to find something they like or in fear that their dreams would not work out. Not because they couldn't afford to do so, but because they are afraid. This fear keeps them trapped in a never ending cycle of unhappiness and missed opportunities.

Personally, I'm in the camp of doing something you dislike even if u struggle with it if it can provide you with some financial security and pay your bills, whilst at the same time pursuing your dreams part time just to test the waters. You have the comfort of a monthly stream of income while also taking a leap of faith and going after what you really want to do in life. And who knows it could work out some day. In the present moment, I'm actually working on many different interests and hobbies. I do the necessary work that i hate but explore other areas that brings me joy, and that is what keeps be going. I have a passion for singing, songwriting, tennis, and making videos like this that not only educates but also aims to bring joy to others. My full-time job only fulfils my bank account while my interests and work that i do on the side fulfils my heart and soul. And who knows, if any one of these side hobbies turn out into something that I can make some money with, hey it's a win win situation now don't you think?

I challenge each and every one of you to go ahead and take a leap of faith. Time waits for no one and you never know when your last day might be. Koby Bryant died suddenly from a helicopter crash at a young age of 41. But I would argue that because he pursued his dreams at a young age, he has already lived a wonderful and fulfilling life as opposed to someone who is too afraid to do what they want and hasn't lived up to their fullest potential despite living until 90. You have also heard of Chadwick Boseman who was immortalised as a great human being who gave it his all despite fighting colon cancer. He pursued his dreams and I bet that he had no regrets that his life had to end earlier than it should. And to Steve jobs, he gave us Apple, the biggest company in the world by pursuing his dream of changing the world and the way we communicate with one another. Without him we wouldn't have all our favourite beloved apple products that we use today. Without him there might not be amazon, google, Facebook because there wouldn't be apps and there wouldn't be devices that people used to do all these things with.

But most importantly, this is about you. How do you want to live your life, and if today was your last day, what would you do differently and how would this carry on to all other areas of your life. Your relationships with your family, your relationship with your friends, your partner. And do you feel fulfilled as a human being or do you feel empty inside. It is never too late to turn your life around and make choices that will make your heart fill with immense joy and gratitude until your life truly ends. So make the decision right now to honour yourself by living your day to the fullest, coz you never know when it might be your last.

Achieving Happiness

Happiness is a topic that is at the core of this channel. Because as humans we all want to be happy in some way shape or form. Happiness strikes as something that we all want to strive for because how can we imagine living an unhappy life. It might be possible but it wouldn't be all that fun no matter how you spin it. However I'm gonna offer another perspective that would challenge the notion of happiness and one that maybe would be more attainable for the vast majority of people.

So why do we as humans search for happiness? It is partly due to the fact that it has been ingrained in us since young that we all should strive to live a happy and healthy life. Happiness has become synonymous with the very nature of existence that when we find ourselves unhappy in any given moment, we tend to want to pivot our life and the current situation we are in to one that is more favourable, one that is supposedly able to bring us more happiness.

But how many of us are actually always happy all the time? I would argue that happiness is not at all sustainable if we were feeling it at full blast constantly. After a while we would find ourselves being numb to it and maybe that happiness would turn into neutrality or even boredom. There were times in my life where i felt truly happy and free. I felt that i had great friends around me, life had limitless possibilities, the weather was great, the housing situation was great, and i never wanted it to end as i knew that it was the best time of my life.

However knowing that this circumstance is only temporary allowed me to cherish each and every moment more meaningfully. As i was aware that time was not infinite and that some day this very state of happiness would somehow end one way or another, that i would use that time wisely and spend them with purpose and meaning. And it was this sense that nothing ever lasts forever that helped me gain a new perspective on everything i was doing at that present moment in time. Of course, those happy times were also filled with times of trials, conflicts, and challenges, and they made that period of my life all the more memorable and noteworthy.

For me, happiness is a temporary state that does not last forever. We might be happy today but sad tomorrow, but that is perfectly okay and totally fine. Being happy all the time is not realistic no matter how you spin it. The excitement of getting a new house and new car would soon fade from the moment you start driving in it, and that happiness you once thought you associated with it can disappear very quickly. And that is okay. Because life is about constant change and nothing really ever stays the same.

With happiness comes with it a whole host of different emotions that aims to highlight and enhance its feeling. Without sadness and sorrow, happiness would have no counter to be matched against. It is like a yin without a yang. And we need both in order to survive.

I believe that to be truly happy, one has to accept that sadness and feelings of unhappiness will come as a package deal. That whilst we want to be happy, we must also want to feel periods of lull to make the experience more rewarding.

I challenge all of you today to view happiness as not something that is static and that once you achieved it that all will be well and life will be good, but rather a temporary state of feeling that will come again and again when you take steps to seek it.

I also want to bring forth to you an alternative notion to happiness, in the form of contentment, that we will discuss in the next video. Take care and I'll see you there.

CPSIA information can be obtained
at www.ICGtesting.com
Printed in the USA
BVHW060822271221
624876BV00013B/687